MASTER
THE ART OF
CONNECTING

LOU DIAMOND

Published by Best Seller Publishing®, Pasadena, CA
Best Seller Publishing® is a registered trademark
Printed in the United States of America.
ISBN-13: 978-1540750136
ISBN-10: 1540750132

This publication is designed to provide accurate and authoritative information with regard to the subject matter covered. It is sold with the understanding that the publisher is not engaged in rendering legal, accounting, or other professional advice. If legal advice or other expert assistance is required, the services of a competent professional should be sought. The opinions expressed by the authors in this book are not endorsed by Best Seller Publishing® and are the sole responsibility of the author rendering the opinion.

Most Best Seller Publishing® titles are available at special quantity discounts for bulk purchases for sales promotions, premiums, fundraising, and educational use. Special versions or book excerpts can also be created to fit specific needs.

For more information, please write:
Best Seller Publishing®
1346 Walnut Street, #205
Pasadena, CA 91106
or call 1(626) 765 9750
Toll Free: 1(844) 850-3500
Visit us online at: www.BestSellerPublishing.org

TABLE OF CONTENTS

INTRODUCTION

I love connecting the dots. Ever since I was a kid, taking a series of unconnected points and linking them together was always fun for me. Whether it was creating an image, completing a drawing of a person or an animal, filling in the details of a scene or outlining the map of a country, connecting the dots always brought me an incredible sense of satisfaction. Partly because I was solving a puzzle, but mostly because the connected dots, to me, seemed to have a greater sense of purpose when I helped bring them together.

Throughout my life and career, it seems I have always been connecting. An outgoing personality, combined with a desire to make connections, has made me the person who seems to know everyone and that combination made the field of sales a natural fit for me. I've always been very good at it. I've made a career selling products and services from the everyday items to luxury ones; from simple financial services to complex multi-currency derivatives; from short-term professional services to multi-year, multi-million-dollar consulting service engagements. I've sold just about everything. And while a career in sales has been a lucrative one at times, I wasn't satisfied that I was connecting all my dots.

I have always found the word "sales" truly shortchanges what it is that I do. Sales are the results of the transactions that I help foster. The sale, however, is only one piece of the puzzle that I am putting together. What I am doing is way more powerful and meaningful than "just" a sale. I am establishing longstanding, trusted relationships that go beyond the sale I am focused on closing.

Whenever I meet someone for the first time and we become better acquainted, I'm not meeting that individual just to close the sale or make the deal; rather, I am always intrigued by each person's unique qualities. I immediately begin to think about whom else I can connect this person with, who could be helpful to them, not only today, but in the future. I contemplate to whom I can introduce this person who would make him or her feel more connected, stronger, confident and powerful than he or she already does. By connecting to individuals or by connecting them to others, I help to develop strong, lasting and powerful relationships. By bringing people together, I help them to grow and develop. This has bigger ramifications and is more worthwhile than just making a sale.

My approach when meeting someone for the first time isn't the typical one. When I meet someone for the first time, I visualize that person in the center of a bubble type of graphic organizer. In each of the bubbles which surround the person, I visualize a series of images and words that this person would use to describe himself or herself. The bubbles contain, for instance, the person's job, contacts, where they grew up, went to school and even where they used to work. When I initially see a person, it's as if all their personal "stats" and "assets" appear in pop-up bubbles around them.

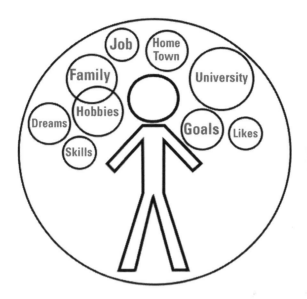

As I get to know them over time, I learn their strengths and weaknesses, likes and dislikes, their goals, their visions and maybe even their dreams. These also become part of my mental visual graphic of the person. And with my innate desire to connect the dots, I can visualize their assets, and I think how I might be able to connect them to another. I envision how I can bring individuals or groups together to help one another.

In the many different sales roles I've had, this is how I viewed my prospects, my clients and my potential partners. It has been a very helpful guide in making me achieve sales targets and goals.

When I thought about this unique way of viewing people and paired it with the sense of enjoyment I get bringing others together, I recognized I needed to share this ability with others. This realization was my inspiration to write this book.

I want to help others succeed, as I have, by adopting this approach. I want people to recognize the power in opening up and sharing information and knowledge with others; that there is incredible value in connecting with others. I have come to realize that my earthly purpose is to inspire amazing people to achieve their dreams and goals, to help them stretch to new heights and to enable people, by connecting with others, to draw out their amazingness so they can perform to their maximum each and every day.

This sense of purpose has led me to coach, mentor and inspire hundreds of leaders and sales professionals. What I have found along this journey is that not everybody sees people the way that I do. Not everyone has the ability to connect one person to another. It puzzled me that not all others saw the value of what I was doing, or appreciated the value of connection as I do. I concluded that some were even afraid to connect with other individuals. I came to recognize that there is actually an art to connection, and it is a skill that can be coached to help others learn to connect.

The relationships and connections that I establish with people are much more powerful than just the one-off transactions. These trust-based connections lead to powerful possibilities to get business deals done faster and to achieve a higher rate of growth than just a regular sale or transaction. My goal in this book is to help you master the art of connecting by establishing deep, lasting, and meaningful connections that will lead to unbridled success in your business, in your career, and in your life.

I have come to recognize, over the course of my career, that most people are not aware that these connections are where business gets done, where the best of the best play, and where the most amazing things happen. This book is a manual to help people get to that space to learn not only how to make a sale, but also how to connect with one another. This book is going to teach you the skills you need to connect the dots.

CHAPTER ONE

BRINGING WORLDS TOGETHER

Several years ago, I was en route to a popular trade show in Las Vegas. My first order of business on arrival was to introduce two connections of mine, Beth and John, who both stood to benefit from meeting one another. Unfortunately, my inbound flight from New York was delayed thirty minutes mid-flight by inclement weather, which we needed to circumvent. At that time, there was no Wi-Fi available on board, so I had no way to inform them that I had been delayed. Neither Beth nor John knew the name of the other, or the context in which I was bringing them together. I was concerned that the opportunity for these two to connect would be missed.

At the scheduled time and place of the meeting, my two connections, Beth and John, walked into a crowded restaurant looking for yours truly. Meanwhile, I was still 30,000 feet in the air above Las Vegas. When I arrived at the restaurant, 45 minutes after our meeting was to have begun, I saw the two of them standing right next to one another. They both smiled when they saw me and gave me a little bit of the "Where the heck were you?" look. Interestingly, neither had spoken a word to the other, despite standing right next to each other for over half an hour.

Beth's company was a startup technology firm based in the northeast. John, at the time, was running an advertising firm in the Midwest. Beth's company had recently grown and was searching for a better marketing and advertising strategy to take it to the next level. John's firm specialized exactly in what Beth's company needed. Both Beth and John were in Las Vegas seeking to increase the services provided by their respective companies and to grow their businesses.

I love this story because there are so many take-aways in this situation. However, there are two specific points that I want to address:

1. What if I had never made it to the restaurant and Beth and John had never connected?
2. I want to highlight the importance of <u>trusted relationships</u> to both Beth and John.

I mentioned earlier that when I see people, I see them within these bubble-like graphic organizers. It's a bit more than that. It's as if I see them as powerful, energizing, growth-infusing connections just awaiting the opportunity to connect. I want to show you how I visualize both Beth and John.

The image above represents Beth. As you can see, there's a sphere around her, with Beth at the core. This imaginary sphere around Beth encapsulates everything that Beth is: her life, her ideas, her goals, her history, her knowledge, her contacts, her strengths, her weaknesses, her personality, her capabilities and her potential. Since Beth is the head of her own technology company, that sphere embodies all the things her company can do as well: its capabilities, its products, its ideas, its vision, its employees, its mission, its goals, etc. As Beth's life and career have grown, so too has the sphere around her.

John also has a sphere around him, demonstrated by the diagram in the next sphere, representing all the things that make up John. Since he runs his own firm as well, the sphere also represents his company and all its capabilities. I like to view these orbs, not so much as spheres, but more like worlds. They represent John's world and Beth's world. Individually, while both worlds are impressive and self-sustaining, together, these are worlds with unlimited potential, which can benefit by connecting with other worlds that can provide strength and growth.

This is how I view people and this is how I view connections. I see the world at large as a series of unique, powerful orbs, just looking to make the right connection. For 30 minutes at a restaurant bar in Las Vegas, Beth and John's worlds were simply staying in their own orbits even though tremendous combined potential was literally inches away. Before I arrived at that restaurant, the combined forces of Beth and John were right there for the taking. Their paths were so close yet neither one of them knew it. Both Beth and John were searching for a way to grow, and making a connection could have been of help to each of them. Yet, it's quite possible had I not arrived, they might have missed the opportunity to connect and capitalize on what each had to offer the other.

While they could see one another physically at the restaurant, without connecting, it's as if they couldn't see the world each represented. Think how often this happens. Every day we cross paths with dozens of people and never actually connect with them. Think how many opportunities are missed everyday by not making a connection with another powerful, energizing, growth-infusing person. Sadly, the connection is never made.

The second point I wanted to address is how important and valuable the trusted relationship meant to both Beth and John. Before I do that, let's address what could have happened in that restaurant if I had not been involved in this equation. Let's say that Beth and John both grabbed a cup of coffee at the restaurant and one of them proactively started a conversation with the other. We can all imagine what this conversation could have sounded like. Here's a dialogue to demonstrate it.

Beth: Are you here for the trade show?

John: Yes I am, how about you?

Beth: I am. It's my first time at this event. Have you been here before?

John: Actually yes, this is my third time. I try to come every year; it's important for my business.

Beth: What is it that you do?

John: I run a marketing and advertising firm. What about you?

Having met hundreds, if not thousands, of people in my life, I will tell you that the above interaction is the most common way people start conversations with complete strangers. A few back and forth questions about one another before they even divulge their names. I've always found it fascinating that people will share what they do for a living before they actually let others know who they are. This hypothetical introduction is how most initial business transactions take place. Instead of a cold call, this is a cold meeting. Visually, it's as if an orbital force of Beth and John's worlds are beginning to take shape. They're both beginning to see a faint outline of each other's world and slowly merge together.

If the conversation were to continue, and both Beth and John learned progressively more about each other, it's as if they'd be able to get a glimpse into each other's worlds. For example, what each of their companies is about, what they specialize in, and how large their businesses are. Both Beth and John would be gauging and measuring each other's businesses to determine whether they could benefit one another. If they're not ready to open up and connect with one another in this cold situation, maybe the encounter ends at this point.

Yet, if there is some spark of a connection, business cards might be exchanged, or they might plan to meet up later at the conference or set up a call for a later date to discuss doing business. After which both parties will do the appropriate follow-up and due diligence. There's a possibility, given more time, these worlds will begin to overlap and start to make a connection.

Let's revisit what actually happened years ago when I finally arrived at that restaurant and helped connect Beth and John. To give some background, Beth and I met through a mutual friend in college. Beth had hired me and my team to help with some business strategy and sales development work. We were very successful in helping her to raise money, get initial clients and come up with a strategy for her business. Beth continues to remain my coaching client to this day. Years ago, John used to work for me at a different company, on my sales team, before he headed out to start his own business.

The diagram above displays visually both my relationship with Beth and with John. As you can see, our worlds are overlapping. I am deeply familiar with both of their worlds as they are with mine. I know why they each do what they do, and how they do it. I'm aware of their capabilities, strengths, and weaknesses, as well as those of each company. I know what they do great and what they need to improve. With this amazing, longstanding connection, we built trust with one another. It's a relationship that took years to establish. They're not just contacts of mine; maintaining a strong relationship throughout the years has made each of them strong and powerful connections. This raises my second point about the need and importance of trusted relationships.

On the flip side, they have an understanding of my world: Why I do what I do, how I do it and what I'm about. In this way, they have benefited from connecting with me. Being able to view their worlds allowed me to recognize that there was a chance that they could help one another. As our meeting began, I ran through how I knew both Beth and John and they both felt comfortable enough in the setting to share more about themselves, to open up and let each other know why they do what they do and what their goals and dreams were.

Being a *trusted connector* enhanced so many elements of this initial meeting. Both Beth and John felt very comfortable sharing and allowing the other to come into the other's circle. Visually, our three worlds were brought together in this overlapping space where everything happens faster. I call this area the Gold Zone. It's a place where powerful connections enable business, growth and opportunity to reach a new level.

It's where the combined strengths and capabilities of each world work together in harmony and where great ideas take place.

Here, the elements of trust, knowledge, gratitude and best intention are aligned to help us all – me, Beth and John – in the same space. It's a great sandbox to play in. It's where the most amazing opportunities exist. It's a hard place to find. So, what happened to Beth and John?

After our meeting, they continued to bond and to learn more about one another. That initial meeting with Beth and John kicked off the relationship between their two worlds. Beth hired John's firm to develop marketing strategies for Beth, which really helped her company's growth. In addition, Beth has referred John's firm to numerous companies. They continue to work together and they each consider each other a strong connection. It truly has been a joy for me to see both the growth and success of each company.

We don't always have the luxury of having a trusted connector to draw out our world powers. Therefore, we must learn how to make powerful connections on our own. We need to be able to learn how to visualize and see the world of others. To begin, we need to ask ourselves one simple question: Am I ready to connect?

CHAPTER TWO

ARE YOU READY TO CONNECT? BUILDING A STRONG CONNECTING CORE

A few years ago after work, a buddy of mine asked me to join him at the gym to play in his Tuesday night basketball game.

Thinking I was still 18, I said yes. I stepped on the court, thinking I was ready to play. Then I was hit with a harsh reality. I was in absolutely awful physical shape. I'd been spending too many hours at a desk and not taking care of my body the way I should. After just a few times up and down the court, I was winded, weak and completely upset with myself. I was physically getting beat by every player I attempted to guard. In addition, I could not have been more ineffective with the offensive part of my game. Simply put, I was sucking wind and sucked in how I played.

After nearly puking on the court, my friend recommended that I start working out with the trainer he used. This trainer was a former boxer who utilizes many boxing training exercises which form an intense workout. I signed up to train with him immediately after my Tuesday night hoops fiasco. His entire workout is like preparing for a fight. The workout consists of a punishing regimen including pushups, sit-ups, squats, punching combinations, jabbing at a heavy bag, moving around within a boxing ring, two and a half straight minutes punching the speed bag, and jumping rope. Anyone who grew up loving the Rocky movies as much as I did would appreciate training like this.

Almost every exercise was focused on core strengthening, and man did I need that. From my initial feeble attempts at pushups, sit-ups, pull-ups, running, and squats, it was evident my core had been neglected for a long, long time. And while I wasn't specifically training for a fight or a race or even a marathon, I wanted to be able to take on any physical activity that I desired and this all started with strengthening my core.

I'll share with you that after a few months of these workouts, everything felt better. I felt stronger all over, more flexible, more able and ready to take on whatever activity I set out to do. My newly strengthened core enabled me to be up for anything that came my way.

Looking back, it is almost comical that I thought I could step right onto the basketball court in a competitive situation without working on getting into shape and strengthening my core. The same could be said about stepping forward to try and make connections to grow your business.

Making powerful connections is hard work, and in some ways, no different than strengthening your physical core. In order to help you make powerful connections, I want to introduce you to the concept of strengthening your *connecting core*.

Over the next few pages I'm going to use some diagrams. I want to shift gears away from the story of Beth and John and talk about someone you should think and care about most, and that's YOU.

This diagram is a circle like the ones in the previous chapter, but you are at the center of this one:

The circle above represents you and all your strengths, characteristics, abilities, contacts and incredible things that you can contribute to this world. It illustrates how your world exists and how it connects to other worlds around you. We're looking at you and your readiness to connect with others.

For context and simplicity, I want to focus on your professional life and making connections in this arena. Just like Beth and John at that trade show in Vegas, you want to grow your business, increase your sales, and grow your customer base. Let's visualize the ideal way of connecting with targets that will help you grow your business.

Next to the image of you will be an image of your targets:

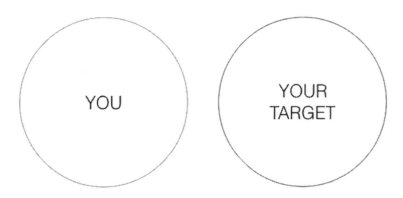

Your targets can be individuals, decision makers or even groups of people within a company or an organization. For our example, let's identify this target as the decision maker at a business that you would like to sell a product or service to.

Now, if this was just a one-off transaction, where you're trying to make just one sale, we wouldn't need a very deep connection would we? The two circles would probably just touch each other, almost right at the edge there.

You would offer what you have to your target and, if needed, a sale can be made. I would like to clarify that this is not really connecting. This is transacting. Think of checking out at a supermarket or at a shopping mall. Going in to buy something at a store is a one-off transaction; you buy it and you're done.

Now let's say you're looking at your target to be more of a strategic partner, someone with whom you're looking to do business for a very long time. Someone who will not only help grow your business, but your combined relationship will help the target as well. Cultivating a long-standing, powerful connection is much preferable than just a tangential connection. You are going to need to know a lot more about your target and they in turn are going to need to know a lot more about you.

The target is going to need a view into why you're in business and what you're all about. You are also going to have to be open and willing to cater to the needs of your target. Your connection should resemble molecules bonding together with a dual purpose of helping one another. This target is your very valuable and important client.

I'm going to show you this transaction in the ideal world.

The ideal world shows that you and your target are so familiar with one another that these overlapping circles are almost inseparable. So how do we get to this point? How do we get to the point where we feel comfortable enough to establish that type of transparency with the targets you pursue?

This next image removes the TARGET piece and focuses on just YOU for a moment:

First, examine yourself. We're going to look at the circle of you to determine the four things that you need to work on to help strengthen your connecting core. You need to enhance your ability to draw in those targets, to actually see deeply into your target and understand them really well. The image below displays what comprises your connecting core:

Through a lifetime of connecting and helping others to do the same, these particular components have been proven to enable you to draw in targets from all different walks of life. Strenghtening your connecting core is going to require you to work on these components that I will coach you on over the next few chapters.

We want you to be able to get to the point that when you are physically ready to go play basketball, you know your body is in shape and you know you're ready. This is the same mindset I need you to have when it comes to connecting.

Situations will arise in which you won't be able to make a great connection with your target if you aren't strong in these four core elements. You might actually dissuade a target from ever working with you. If you approach somebody and you are not authentic, you might be seen as an unworthy distraction. If you approach an opportunity hesitantly, fearful and unconfident, that fear could be perceived by the target as a lack of capability. You may never make the connection that's needed to help grow your business and in turn help theirs as well.

Another notable element essential to a person's connecting core is the ability to be empathetic. If you go to connect and you don't care about your targets, you're only concerned about yourself and you don't listen properly to what they have to offer, then why would they want to get into your circle and into your world?

This is the first quality we'll be dealing with in the next chapter. I'm going to highlight the skills needed to build a strong connecting core. A strong connecting core will set you up for success, not only in business, but also in life.

CHAPTER THREE

STRENGTHENING YOUR CONNECTING CORE: THE POWER OF EMPATHY

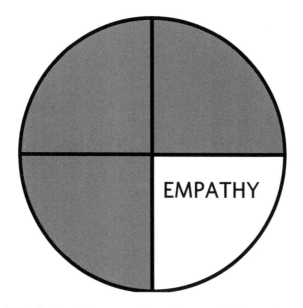

In the fall of 2014, I received a phone call from the CEO of a mid-sized technology firm, Amanay Technologies. The CEO was having issues closing new business and wanted me to work with the sales team and assess where they were coming up short. Five years earlier, Amanay launched on to the scene with a great deal of early success and was highly regarded in the cloud computing technology business. Amanay was at the forefront of internet technology. However, after three years of growth, their revenue seemed to plateau.

I met with the CEO and the head of sales and received a briefing on the company's vision and goals. They had an impressive client roster, and a very polished and professional sales team with years of experience. The company gave me a walkthrough of all their capabilities, including a demonstration of the services Amanay provides. They also showed me the sales presentation that they were slated to give to a new prospect the very next day. I asked if it would be possible for me to attend that meeting to observe the sales team in action to get a better of idea of where their efforts might be falling short. They were delighted to have me attend the sales meeting with the Amanay sales team.

The next morning, as I observed, an Amanay team of three – a sales person, an account manager, and a person from the technology team – made their presentation to the prospect. At this point, I want to share the conversation that took place afterward among the team on the car ride back to Amanay's offices.

Account Manager: "We crushed that meeting."

Sales Lead: "I think that went great, don't you?"

Tech Guy: … (Okay, well the tech guy said nothing because he was laser focused on catching up on the 40 emails he had gotten during the sales meeting.)

When we got back to the office, I met again with the CEO and Head of Sales. They had already gotten an email from the presentation team stating that it had been a "good meeting" in the view of the Sales Lead. They asked me to relate my thoughts and whether I shared the same enthusiasm as the pitch team.

I did not.

In the hundreds, if not thousands of sales meetings I've attended in my life, I will never forget the way this one began. I want to be clear to you, the reader, that this is an example of what **not** to do and how **not** to have a sales meeting.

At the presentation, the Sales Lead stood in front of the room, got his PowerPoint presentation up and ready, failed to even acknowledge and say hello to anyone in the room, and then opened with the following statement:

> *"I am so excited with what WE have accomplished at Amanay and how WE are changing the entire landscape of cloud computing and the internet. OUR technology is groundbreaking and is so far ahead of our competition. WE will share OUR latest release of OUR software today. Afterwards, it will be clear to see why WE are the obvious choice."*

This was the first meeting with the prospect; their first exposure to Amanay. In his presentation, the sales lead managed to go through the first 10 slides using only the Amanay name or the pronouns I, we, our and us. In addition, he completed the entire presentation without asking the prospect a single question. In fact, he never asked the prospects' names, what they did, or gave them any opportunity to speak.

I remember my brain was spinning on the ride back to Amanay's offices. I couldn't decide if I was more shocked by how they went through an entire sales pitch only talking about themselves, or by the fact that they somehow thought that the meeting went well. The sales team forgot the most important rule when it comes to sales: The only thing that matters is the client.

The Power of Empathy

em•pa•thy (noun): the psychological identification with, or vicarious experiencing of, the feelings, thoughts, or attitudes of another.

Not surprisingly, the Amanay sales team failed to connect with their prospective client. There was no follow-up sales meeting; there was no revenue generated. There was only a missed opportunity to connect. How can you connect if you have no understanding of your prospect? All of Amanay's sales materials, mindset, and communication style was focused on themselves.

Remember, this was a first meeting — a first opportunity. All Amanay did in that presentation was to **TELL** the clients about themselves, never ASKING what the prospect needed. If you think about your world and the target's world (like in the image of the two circles), it's as if Amanay only laid out their own world. We can see clearly the circle depicting Amanay, but it's as if the target's world circle is invisible to Amanay. It makes it impossible for Amanay to see how they could possibly connect with this client because they never bothered to ask or give the target an opportunity to describe its own world.

A good sales person is not only able to understand the world the prospective client lives in, but is also a great **connector** who can feel the client's pain, because the salesperson is so connected to the target's world. A connector can empathize with everything the target is going through and what it's like to walk in the client's shoes. While we can assume what some of the problems are that the target is experiencing, and your company may have the greatest technology solutions, the best pitches, the best sales team, the most incredible capabilities possible, if you do not **ask** the client what they need, you're never going to be able to help them. Nor will they want you to.

In our first exercise of strengthening our connecting core, we need to flex our **empathy** muscles. We need to put aside our matters to be able to understand what matters to the client. To strengthen the connecting core, we need to go a place of "ASK and LISTEN." When it came to the Amanay team in that pitch, all they did was "TELL and TALK."

ASK

ASK VS. TELL

	KNOW	DON'T KNOW
ASK		
TELL		

The chart above highlights the Ask and Tell matrix. This is one of the most essential matrices that we use in performance coaching. Initially, this matrix is blank. It's used to understand what way is best for communicating with clients, targets or others. It's a format for understanding what type of individuals fall into each of these boxes. For example, the Tell and Know boxes would contain those career types such as teachers, lawyers, doctors and other professionals who have studied in a systematic way to achieve their careers. They are educated people from whom one can learn just by listening.

ASK VS. TELL

	KNOW	DON'T KNOW
ASK		
TELL	Teacher Doctor Professional	

If I move over to the other side of the matrix and look at the Tell Don't Know box, what falls in there? You see inside it I've placed the words "blow-hard boss." That is the kind of person, we joke, who tells you something that he or she thinks they know, but really doesn't know. There are plenty of people that do this all the time; they tell us what to do. While these are authorities, it's not as powerful in a learning environment to come from this place. While one may be authoritative, the reality is that another is not as receptive to learn in this space. Think about when you were first in school; you took at face value everything your teacher said. As you grew older, you began to think independently and didn't necessarily accept everything you were taught. In the professional business environment, this matrix sometimes comes off too harshly and is perhaps not the place to come to from the Tell side of the equation.

ASK VS. TELL

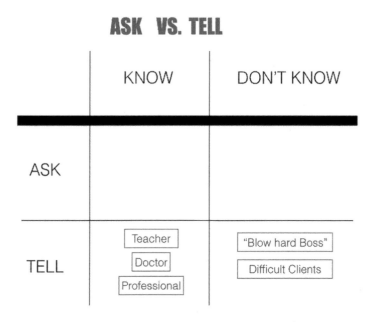

	KNOW	DON'T KNOW
ASK		
TELL	Teacher Doctor Professional	"Blow hard Boss" Difficult Clients

Let's move to the Ask bucket. When it comes to Ask and Know or Ask and Don't Know, what types of people do we know who fall into each of these? By the way, everyone always thinks of parents first when they go to this bucket. Parents can stretch across both boxes because they sometimes ask and they know what they're telling you about. For example, who left the toilet seat up? Obviously, when mothers ask this question, they already know the answer, especially in a household with only one male. In some cases, when they ask certain questions, they really don't know the answer. When they come from that place, it requires the person being asked the question to respond and get involved in the conversation.

What other people live in this Ask and Know space? Many people say therapists. They ask questions to understand what is bothering a person or keeping a person down. They want to know what issues a person would like to move forward from. Consultants also fall into this bucket. Many business consultants ask questions surrounding what the business is about. In some cases, they already know the answers, but in many cases, just by asking they come from a more powerful place because they're considering the client's needs. They're asking because they want to hear what the client values.

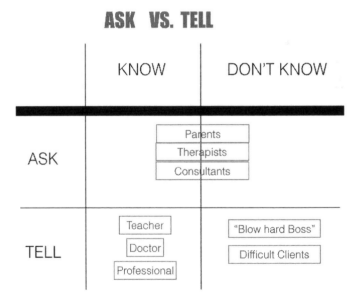

ASK VS. TELL

	KNOW	DON'T KNOW
ASK		Parents Therapists Consultants	
TELL	Teacher Doctor Professional	"Blow hard Boss" Difficult Clients

Finally, the last great category that we placed in this box is coaches. Coaches live in this space where they're always asking the questions, regardless of whether they know the answers to them or not. Coaches and consultants live in this space too. Within this asking forum is a much more powerful way to communicate. When you are in this Ask Tell matrix and you come from this place of asking, you are taking the client's view into consideration. In fact, you are making the client the focus; you are empathizing with your client.

ASK VS. TELL

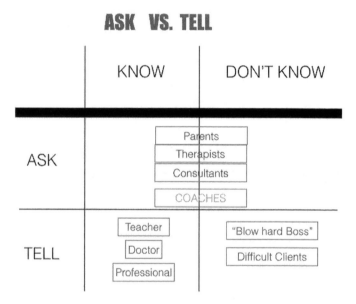

So, our first step when it comes to the powerful place of being empathetic and stretching that connector muscle is to come from a place where we ask questions. Asking clients what they need, what things are holding them back, and how you can help them comes from this point. Imagine if Amanay had started their meeting in an asking forum and how much more powerful it would have been. Rather than telling them things Amanay *thinks* the target needs and why they *think* the target should have taken a certain action, it is better not to speculate. The client is much more receptive when they're being *asked* about what concerns them.

Great sales and great connections are made when you come from "ASK." Great connectors drown out the world around them and focus on the needs of the target. Great coaches are great listeners.

What does it really mean to be a great listener? What do we mean by listening? To get a better understanding of the term, we'll examine what many executive coaches describe as the 3 Levels of Listening.

LISTEN

Level 1, which is called internal listening, is "It's all about me!" How everything relates to me. We do this about 98% of the time. We relate everything as it happens to ourselves. In fact, while you were reading this, your initial reaction was probably to think to yourself, *There's no way I relate things to myself 98% of the time!* Odds are I proved my point.

Level 2 is focused listening. It's all about the person on whom you are focused. It's as if there is a hardwired connection one to another, such that the distractions and the noise of the outside world cease to exist. Listening Level 2 is where coaching resides. This is where we're very focused on a certain individual and what they're about. This is a great place to begin when it comes to being an effective and strong connector.

Level 3 is global listening. It is a soft focus on another, where one is aware of the whole environment and has a deep understanding and intuition. It's like your radar, sonar, or chakra; senses are all on high alert. Listening Level 3 enables you to read the room. As you become more connected to the client, you sense when things are right and when they aren't. In that sales meeting with Amanay, I not only was in Listening Level 2, hearing the Amanay sales lead go on and on about how great their company was, I was also in Listening Level 3, sensing that the client was as surprised as I that Amanay didn't focus the attention of this meeting on the client. They were not only uninterested; after a little while they were fed up with the Amanay team. It was visible on their faces, in their body language, and in their eye contact or lack thereof.

LEVELS OF LISTENING

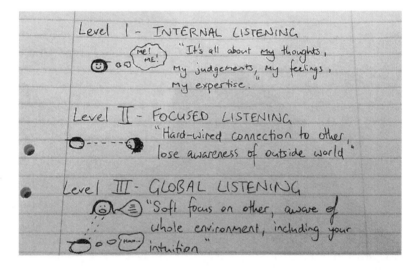

Level 1 - INTERNAL LISTENING
(ME!) (ME!) "It's all about my thoughts, my judgements, my feelings, my expertise."

Level II - FOCUSED LISTENING
"Hard-wired connection to other, lose awareness of outside world"

Level III - GLOBAL LISTENING
"Soft focus on other, aware of whole environment, including your intuition"

The client was fed up with Amanay not only making the meeting about itself, but it turned them off quite quickly. Amanay did not come from a place where they were asking nor were they in the right listening level.

If you've tried to do a Google search for Amanay while reading this, you probably did not find a cloud computing company with this name. The alias, AMANAY, was an acronym I used to highlight that this firm was all "about me and not about you."

While it is a real company, I nicknamed the project I worked on with them *Amanay*. The goal was to get the staff to a place where they flipped the name around so they would become ACANAM, *all about the CLIENT and not about me*. Coming from a place where you ask the client or target questions enables them to recognize that you are listening to them, and that you care about what they are about. You can see their world and everything they encompass. Since 98% of the time we're in Listening Level 1, our clients love to hear about themselves. Therefore, by listening to them and focusing on them, you're catering to where they are most comfortable, talking about themselves. They don't ever need to hear about your capabilities or your latest achievements; all that needs to be focused on is what you are going to do for them.

The power of empathy within your connected core is made stronger by asking and listening. If the Amanay meeting is an example of what not to do, what are some of the ideal ways to be empathetic and strengthen your connecting core when going after targets? Every initial encounter with a target or prospect should begin by asking as many questions as possible. Ask what has been going well for them and what has not; ask what their pain points are, ask what would make their lives easier, their jobs easier, and ask why they do what they do. All of these asks begin to help shape your target's world for you. You begin to gain an understanding from their perspective on what they're all about, not from any preconceived notions you may have had.

Listening is not only done with your ears. Great connectors know that when it comes to listening, you need to listen with all of your senses.

Observe the body language of your targets. As you ask questions, see how people react. Watch how they move; see how they position themselves. Not everyone is going to open up right away; it takes time to establish trust, so read how people react in these early stages. People love talking about their own world, so 98% of the time, they're going to make it about themselves. Since you're asking questions about them, you'll be able to learn a tremendous amount just by listening and observing reactions. It will help you direct the conversation toward areas of interest to the target. If you observe that someone is uncomfortable, uncertain, closed off or unwilling to open up and share, address that person directly and ask what they'd like to learn about. Then observe their physical response and notice if it changes. It may not, however, but by being aware of someone's physical body language and trying to address it, you may begin to start connecting and have a better understanding of that individual.

When you have an entire sales presentation or pitch that's ready to be unleashed, it's the last thing you should be worried about. If you're concerned about your sales materials, presentation, PowerPoint or demonstration, you are not focusing on the client and you are not utilizing your power of empathy. Great connectors utilize their power of empathy by being sensitive and aware of the target's needs. You need to come from the "Ask" quadrant and stay in Listening Levels 2 and 3.

Make this a habit with all your existing and possible connections. When you do, you're on your way to becoming a powerful connector by utilizing your power of empathy.

Flexing Your Connecting Core
The power of empathy on its own can win you business.

I was the head of business development for a digital agency and one of our clients was Compaq Computers. Compaq had decided they needed to overhaul their entire online presence and spent months pulling together a complex and incredibly intricate 'RFP' (Request for a Proposal). The purpose of the RFP was to select an agency that would oversee and manage the entire project. The project was going to be a massive undertaking and would require a great deal of resources, months of work, tremendous coordination of multiple teams and agencies, and most importantly, it would mean a great deal of revenue for our company.

After weeks of late nights and working with many different groups throughout our company, we came back with a well thought-out, economically efficient, technically sound and design-savvy proposal – as did 15 other firms vying for this job.

After two months of sifting through all the responses of all the agencies, Compaq said they had narrowed down their selection to five agencies and that we were one of them. We were to fly down and present our proposal to the 25-member decision-making body in Houston later that month.

A month after learning we made it to the final grouping, a team headed to Texas comprised of our company's CEO, COO, head of design, head of engineering and me. We also learned that we were going to be the *last* group to present that day, and that we had up to two hours to present.

The night before the pitch, our team gathered in a hotel room in Houston as we laid out how we would present to this group: I'd kick off the meeting, introduce the team and then each member would run through a certain aspect of their team's expertise and how we would apply our methodology and process to make Compaq's website everything they'd ever want it to be.

I remembered I didn't sleep very well that night. I knew that (a) we needed to stand out, and (b) going dead last was not going to work in our favor. After 8+ hours of four other agencies' presentations, I was fairly certain the decision-making group wouldn't absorb anything we would say to them.

As the hour approached, I peeked into the room we were to present in and saw 25 people who looked like they either needed a drink or a nap. They were completely fried. I could actually feel how tired and frustrated they were from such a long day of hearing and seeing so many pitches. I looked at our team…and decided to make a change.

I huddled them around and said to them: "Hey guys, forget the pitch. My gut is telling me that we have to do something 'off the reservation' to make this work."

The five of us entered the room – which looked like a university lecture hall – and stood in front of the group.

I said, "Thank you for having us here today. I know you're completely exhausted from a full day of pitches from our competition. I'm going to make it easy for you and let you wrap up your day fairly quickly. You have our proposal in front of you. We're committed to working with you to make Compaq's site what you want it to be. We've brought our CEO here to show you that the whole company is behind this effort. And we know that we're more than capable of being the agency you can count on. We know you'll be extremely happy when you select us as your digital agency of record. At this point, if you have any specific questions about our proposal we're here to answer them for you."

The room was mostly silent, until one of the decision makers from IT asked a technical question that he had. Our head of engineering stepped forward and answered the question right on the spot.

After his response, the room was still quiet, I then followed with, "Are there any more questions for us?"

With no comments from anyone else in the room, I concluded with, "We thank you for giving us your time and we look forward to getting started soon."

The five of us exited the room in under two minutes. We crammed into the rental car and headed to the airport.

Two thoughts went through my head as we were driving to Houston's International Airport:

I couldn't believe that I just did that...and I was probably going to be fired. As I was second guessing myself, my phone rang. It was the head of marketing from Compaq. I remember literally shaking as I answered the call.

"Lou?" she inquired, "I just called because it seems one member of your team left a briefcase here in the conference room."

It turns out the COO was so startled at how quickly we finished the presentation he forgot his bag.

She continued, "Would you like me to mail it back to your New York office or would you like to turn around, come back here to get it and while you're here sign the contract to be our new Digital Agency of Record? Congratulations!"

The only words that came out of my mouth at that moment were, "Turn the car around!"

My power of empathy was even more in tune than it was before the pitch, because I could feel the internal screams and excitement from everyone on our team within that rental car as we spun the car around and returned to Compaq's HQ.

Over a few glasses of champagne paired with many sighs of relief, one of the members of the selection committee made a comment I'll never forget: "Many thought you were crazy to not deliver your pitch, but I thought that if your team was aware enough to know exactly how we were feeling, then imagine how well they'll work with us. This considerate and adaptive team is exactly who we want to hire."

Here's to the power of empathy and how important it is to really LISTEN to your target.

CHAPTER FOUR

YOUR CONNECTING CORE: THE FEARLESS MINDSET

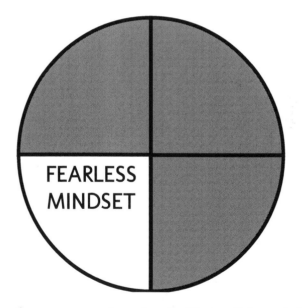

FEARLESS MINDSET

As a performance coach and a facilitator, I have led many workshops attended by some incredibly talented sales individuals and leaders. These workshops are usually held at an off-site location to step away from the everyday routine of work. The attendees are focused on improving how they sell and connect. At one workshop for a midsize company, I received a list of attendees from the head of sales. When the workshop began, I noticed that one individual listed was not present. His name was Michael Thomas.

After an amazing and productive workshop, I returned to the company about a week later to have a debriefing session with the head of sales. The purpose was to recap how the workshop went, discuss some of the findings and breakthroughs identified and select things we could work on in the future. As our discussion continued, the head of sales asked me how Michael Thomas performed during the workshop. When I shared with him that Thomas was a no-show, the head of sales was surprised. He popped out of his chair and looked around the office to find him. After locating him, he brought him into our meeting. Thomas had no idea who I was. The head of sales then began to speak to him.

"Michael, I understand that you were NOT at the workshop last week."

Michael replied, "I had a personal matter to attend to."

The best part about being a great connector with a strong connecting core is that my empathy muscles are fine tuned. This means I have excellent listening skills and a fantastic ability to detect bullshit and lies immediately.

The head of sales sensed exactly what I did at that moment: Michael was talking out of his ass. He looked guilty as sin and became nervous as he began to decode that I was the person who ran the workshop.

Prior to the workshop, all the participants had received some pre-workshop materials and information to help them prepare for it. Michael had emailed me about what we would cover during the workshop. Among the list of included topics was how to improve your sales, getting out of your comfort zone, and many other communication skills, including public speaking.

Michael Thomas dreaded public speaking. So much so, that on the day of the workshop, with the thought of having to address his fear of public speaking, he couldn't even get out of bed. He literally could not face the day. Scrolling through his email folders, the head of sales saw a message in his inbox dated the morning of the workshop. He had overlooked it until our meeting. It was from Michael Thomas saying that he wasn't feeling well and wouldn't be attending the workshop. Michael's boss then inquired, "So Michael, was it a personal matter or sickness that kept you from the workshop?" A really great and relevant question.

Over the last several years, I've interviewed more than 250 CEOs and heads of sales, and among other questions, I always ask them to list the biggest sales challenges they face. The most common answers to that question are:

Networking

Building the pipeline

Connecting to the senior decision makers

Discussing price

Closing faster

During follow-up interviews with many of these leaders, I've tried to better understand the specific issues of these sales challenges within several different industries. There is one common element at the root of all these sales issues: FEAR.

The truth is that I used to believe fear was not real. I considered that it was merely a sign of weakness or something conjured up in our brain based on a learned behavior. I was wrong.

If you were to ask Michael Thomas, he would tell you that fear is very real.

Fear kept him from coming to the workshop that day. The fear that public speaking was going to be even discussed during the workshop scared him to the extent that he avoided coming into work that day. Michael even sent an email to his boss that he was sick. He also experienced fear when he got caught in a lie when his boss confronted him about whether he was sick or dealing with a personal matter.

Fear is real and we all face it every single day.

Through all the performance workshops I have facilitated, I've addressed and investigated fears to try to identify the things that hold people back. Fear can be paralyzing, making it impossible for a person to accomplish anything. The example of Michael Thomas not being able to leave his home, attend work or even participate in the workshop is an extreme case, but sometimes that's what fear can do to us.

There are many fears that confront a person in business. You may be afraid of failing; afraid that you'll be rejected; afraid that people won't like you; afraid that when you enter a meeting that you might be too young, or too old; afraid that maybe people will find out that you're not as good as you think you are. All of these are legitimate issues that I have seen manifest in sales and business people over the years.

There are so many fears that affect us as human beings in our personal lives that they are very likely to carry over into our professional lives. There is no such thing as a "nine to five" job anymore. Our personal lives have overlapped so much with our work lives that there is no longer a clear line of demarcation separating the two. Throw in the wonders of modern technology with things like email, voicemail, cell phones, texting and access to the internet make work and personal life completely intertwined.

Therefore, the personal feelings and fears we feel outside of work can affect what our work day is like, and vice versa.

A bad work day can be brought right into the home. In both places we carry over a lot of fear we've had in our lives, which can result in not only physical changes, but also will cause us to come up with numerous excuses and to create other limiting beliefs that will prevent us from doing what we should. I address fear in the workshops which I often lead. The participants and I discuss their fears in depth. We go into a level of detail that really helps us understand the personal nature of what fear can do.

For some people, fears can bring about a feeling of physical discomfort and stress. I've witnessed people getting sick to their stomach as they contemplate the fears they have. Some will feel physical pangs in their neck and shoulders; frequently, others experience migraines.

As you read this now, you're probably thinking about fears that you have had whenever you've been in a really uncomfortable situation. You may have been sick to the point that you couldn't move, couldn't even get out of bed. Just like Michael.

When it comes to the top fears experienced in sales, you'll see below what sales people go through. Fear affects our personal lives emotionally and that carries over directly into how we sell. The following fears about sales have been experienced by just about every single person throughout a sales career:

AFRAID THEY'LL SAY NO.

Without a doubt, rejection and hearing NO is one of the worst and the most common fear that sales people face.

Think about what takes place: You prepare for a meeting; you set up a chance to present your capabilities, tell people what you do, and try and pitch what you have to offer. You are truly putting yourself out there and exposing yourself. Obviously, you're hoping to win the business. Even the possibility of hearing a NO sends chills up some people's spine. So much so that if someone says to you, "We'll get back to you," and you have an action to try to proactively follow-up with that client, you might be reluctant to do so because you're so afraid you'll ultimately hear the word NO.

AFRAID THEY'LL SAY YES.

This is a very popular fear amongst entrepreneurs. This is also related to the FEAR OF SUCCESS. After you've presented your capabilities or displayed your product to a TARGET, there's this feeling that hits you of being overwhelmed. "What if they do say yes?" "What will I do then?" "How can I handle this new business?" "Will I be able to deliver on what I promised?" Sometimes hearing "YES, I want to do business with you" is equally, if not more, terrifying that hearing "NO." This fear relates directly to letting people down and the FEAR OF DISAPPOINTMENT.

THEY WON'T TAKE ME SERIOUSLY.

This fear is a very common one with young professionals who have either just entered the workforce or have just begun working at a new organization. When you go into that important meeting or you get in front of a large group, there is a fear that runs through sales people that they won't be taken seriously. They'll think that people will view them as a joke, that people will feel they're too inexperienced, and this can lead to issues where people won't attempt to set up those bigger meetings. It will literally limit the opportunity that potentially awaits them.

ASKING FOR THE BUSINESS.

This is one of my favorite fears to address and it is probably the most common fear in sales. I find it fascinating that people around the globe will set out to pitch their product or service; they'll put together elaborate sales and marketing materials; they'll customize solutions for specific targets; they'll deliver a top-notch, professional sales pitch… and NEVER ACTUALLY ASK FOR THE BUSINESS! It's as if they assume that the target completely understands that by learning about the capabilities of a seller, that it means the seller actually wants their business. This inability to ASK for the business you'd like to take on is directly related to the fear of rejection. By ASKING for the business you're opening the door for the target to say NO.

THE FEAR OF TALKING ABOUT PRICE.

Larger companies and more established businesses have pretty much set the market on what a certain price should be. Therefore, younger companies, newer industries and services, newer technologies, or even personal service businesses face a huge challenge, especially for entrepreneurs, when it comes to pricing the value of what you do. I've heard sales presentations in which people talk about all the great things they'll do for one another and price is never mentioned. The target will have no idea of cost to obtain these services. Granted some might use this as a tactic to engage the target to ask, "What does this cost if I want to work with you?" However, in most instances, price is a feared topic that many avoid as there is a belief that the amount will kill the entire sale. The conversation of price is so scary that people waiver on amount. They'll push an opportunity to the backburner while they try and figure out what the right price will be. The fear of talking about price has probably hurt ongoing business in the long run.

THE FEAR OF BEING PERCEIVED AS TOO SALESY OR SLEAZY.

"Sales" has a terrible rap; even the word *sleazy* is actually a derivative of the word *sale*. It comes off as that cheesy, pushy, uncomfortable type of person who is only focused on the sale and only focused on themselves. A term I love when it comes to the word *sleazy* is "commission breath": that feeling that you're dealing with a sales person who is only interested in you to close the sale. Usually, they've had several cups of coffee and a few cigarettes and are so aggressive that it feels as if they're shoving the sale down your throat. That's the image many people have when they think of sales people. Some people are so afraid of being perceived as sleazy, even though their main function is sales, that they try and conceal that they are in sales.

Once I attended a sales conference and saw a business card that actually read, "Top Line Revenue Manager." The fact that we were at a sales conference wasn't mentioned, nor was the fact that the person was actually in sales. He didn't put it on his business card because he didn't want to be identified as a sales person. Other people sometimes include adjectives before the word sales in their business cards to imply that they're not "just" a sales person. For example, "I'm an institutional sales person." "I'm a corporate development sales person." All of these titles amount to wasted effort because there is such a fear of being linked to that terrible image of being in "sales" and the fear of being perceived as "just a sales person."

THE FEAR OF BEING PERCEIVED AS TOO PUSHY.

Everyone needs a little bit of push here or there, but there's always a concern of coming across as too aggressive. Some sales people are so afraid to move forward or being perceived as too pushy because they want a stronger relationship or connection with their target that they fail just because of their fear.

FEAR OF FAILURE.

The granddaddy of all fears. It's also the most common fear in every organization. The fear of failing, of letting people down, specifically of letting down those people who regularly depend on you – your parents, your spouse, your children, your boss, your co-workers, and others. The fear of failure is the one that keeps rising to the top of the list of all fears. Yet most interestingly, as a coach, the fear of failure is sometimes the hardest one to unearth.

A FEARLESS MINDSET

While fears are very real and confront us every day, most people don't realize that they do not have to control our lives and limit us from achieving our goals and dreams. Think of the amazing potential you would have if you lived a life free of debilitating fears. Who wouldn't want to have a FEARLESS MINDSET that you could activate to clear through the obstacles that are impediments on your path toward greatness?

To help strengthen your connecting core, achieving a fearless mindset is integral to becoming a Master Connector. I want to be clear. This way of thinking is not about ignoring your fears and pretending they do not exist. Rather, it's the exact opposite. It's about knowing what your fears are and how to push through them.

ACHIEVING A FEARLESS MINDSET STEP 1: IDENTIFY YOUR FEARS.

When it comes to becoming a great connector with a strong connecting core, we must understand that these fears exist and they're real. So, the first step in establishing a fearless mindset is to identify the fears you have. And by *identifying* I mean actually naming the fear. The ones listed on the previous pages are a few common ones. However, there are others, and it's important to personalize your fear so you can comfortably recognize and own it. Before we begin identifying and naming our fears, it's important to understand the difference between fears and limiting beliefs.

A limiting belief is the not-so-distant cousin of fear. I like to use this example to best explain what limiting beliefs are. Often in sales, we establish a strong relationship with our targets. In fact, there are many people who believe they must be liked by a client before the client will do business with them.

Is this really true? Do we always have to be liked by someone to do business with them? Is being liked by your client a requirement to do business with them?

While in most cases we tend to do business with people who like us, I can pretty much guarantee that not everyone is liked by everyone else. Yet, many sales people believe that they must be liked by the client to make the sale. Having worked on Wall Street for many years, I can attest that there were many people I did business with that didn't like me very much. Neither did I always like those with whom I did business.

So, the belief that one must be liked by a client to do business with them is a limiting belief. As I like to succinctly state it to those attending the workshops I lead, "FEARS ARE REAL, LIMITING BELIEFS ARE BULLSHIT." To expand and be a little less vulgar: Limiting beliefs are the lies we tell ourselves that are deeply embedded in a FEAR we have.

In this case, "I must be liked by the client" is the limiting belief inside of the "FEAR OF NOT BEING APPRECIATED." By not being liked, you're afraid that the target or client won't appreciate what you can offer his or her business. So, the fear can sometimes mask itself in the form of a limiting belief – in this case, believing that you need to be liked to do business.

And while it's very nice to be liked, it isn't always necessary to close the deal.

A great exercise for sales teams to do is to have a fear identifying session. In that session, listen for limiting beliefs and try to dig down to determine what the underlying fears are that are holding back the team. Limiting beliefs tend to come out in strong declarative statements.

Here are a few of my favorites:

> "I have to be at every meeting to close the deal." →
> (Really? That could be challenging as companies
> begin to grow. Sounds like the FEAR OF LOSING
> CONTROL or LETTING GO.)
>
> "The sales presentation has to be perfect." → (Nothing is
> ever perfect – a direct derivative of FEAR OF FAILURE.)
>
> "I'm too young to meet with the CEO of
> that company." → (FEAR OF NOT BEING
> APPRECIATED.)

You get the idea. Get your whole sales team on board with this and call "BS" when you hear limiting beliefs around the office. This will begin to identify and name the FEAR.

ACHIEVING A FEARLESS MINDSET STEP 2:
MOVE THROUGH THE FEAR INTO COURAGE

Question: How do we do that?

Once you've identified the fear – you now have the fun task to figure out how to move through it. As a performance coach, I can tell you this is not a one-size-fits-all solution. In some cases, moving through this fear can take years of hard work.

What I will say is that every individual is different and the basic approach I'm providing below is a start.

Every time you confront one of your fears, try to "flip the fear on its head." By that I mean take the opposite view. Start out by asking yourself, "Okay, this is the fear I have. What's the opposite side of that fear?"

The following example will best explain this approach.

Moving through AFRAID THEY'LL SAY NO.

If you're afraid the target will say no, consider the possibility that they might say yes. Pick up the phone and actually call the client to get the answer. Speak to the client and ask if there's a chance that you can do business together. You should embrace that fear holding you back of being rejected because the faster you get to no, the more time you can focus on closing the yeses. Let me restate that. Get to "No" faster so you can eventually get more "Yeses."

This philosophy supports the proposition that the minute that you present something, you need to take action so your pipeline doesn't go stale. You should get things off your pipeline and get to the close as quickly as possible. Focus on what you can do to hear the answer sooner. If there's a possible chance you're going to do business, ask.

Ask, "Do you think there's a way that we can do business with one another?" If they come back and say, "This isn't the right time," GREAT, now I can focus on the real opportunities that I can spend time on to move forward. Embrace the fear of that rejection and hearing no. You want to get past the "no" answers because that will enable you to spend the time that's necessary on getting the "yes" answers.

Get the idea? Okay here are a few more fears and how you can move through them to obtain a FEARLESS MINDSET.

Moving through THE FEAR OF ASKING FOR THE BUSINESS.

"If you do not ASK you cannot CLOSE."

If you don't get to the point of asking, "Can we do business together?" or "We would really like to work with you," they don't know that it is what you really want. Let the target know that you're asking for their business. It puts the onus on the target to decide whether they want to work with you. The only way you're ever going to work with someone is to actually ask if you can.

Moving through THE FEAR OF BEING PERCIEVED AS TOO PUSHY.

If you're afraid of being perceived as too pushy, trust me when I tell you that your targets are *expecting* you to sell. They know what your role is. They have their own sales people in their own organizations and would expect them to push. Your targets have dealt with sales reps before. Don't fret that your target is worried that you are being too pushy; the way to spin this fear is to remember that your targets expect you to sell to them.

Moving through THE FEAR OF TALKING ABOUT PRICE.

You're afraid to talk about price? It's important to understand that nothing in life is for free. There's value in everything you do. Don't shortchange yourself. Your value is what they're deciding.

The fear of discussing price is interesting. People tend to discount themselves very quickly because they feel that price is the reason that targets are choosing them. This is yet another limiting belief. It's way more than just the price. There's a whole set of reasons why they're choosing you. Price might be one of the factors, but it's certainly not the only factor. Don't dodge talking about price. Embrace it. Bring it up and represent the value you have, because that's what you're in business to do, and it obviously is the only way to set the bar to begin working with someone. Finally, if you're afraid to sell and you're afraid to face anyone, just remember that everyone fails at times and this time you just might succeed.

When coaches or psychologists discuss the topic of failure, they often bring up the baseball analogy and remind us that the best baseball players, the hall of famers, fail seven out of 10 times. Embrace that concept in everything you do. You're not going to win every sale. You're not going to win every pitch. You're not always going to be the best. There will be others that sometimes will be better, but there's plenty of business out there. In fact, you're going to fail and you should look to fail because those failures are only going to be able to make you stronger in the wins that you do have. When it comes to these fears that you have, accept that they are real. They exist. If you remember that, you know how to move through them into courage and you'll enable your mind to have that fearless mindset.

Remember Michael? Well, after the confrontational meeting in the sales office, I suggested that I would like to talk more with Michael to understand why he was so reluctant to come to the workshop. He eventually shared that he truly was scared to even to address the fact that he was speaking publicly.

He also recognized that he needed improvement in this area, which would lead to improvements in his sales technique.

I worked with Michael for about three months to help him not only with presenting, but also prepping him for his presentations. It turns out it wasn't speaking in public that unnerved Michael Thomas. It was actually that he might be perceived as looking like he didn't know what he was talking about. He was afraid he didn't measure up. He didn't have the Ivy League education that some of his peers did. He didn't have the technology experience that some of the others did at the technology company where he worked. That perception was what he was most afraid of: that people would look at him as an imposter and that they wouldn't take him seriously.

The fact is that Michael is a very polished individual and is one of the top performers for this company. When the head of sales had asked me how Michael Thomas had performed at the workshop, part of his disappointment on learning Michael was a no-show was in the fact that he thought Michael was one of the better, smarter sales people on his team and was a person who the other sales people could learn from. Interestingly, when you look at these fears that paralyzed Michael and kept him in bed that day, you should know that now he recognizes what the fear is, confronts it, and he steps through it.

In his free time, Michael Thomas is now an active member and participant of Toastmasters. He has delivered several speeches within his company and every week provides a status update to his team members. By stepping through his fear to courage, he started to develop that fearless mindset that is essential in making him a great connector.

CHAPTER FIVE

YOUR CONNECTING CORE: THE POWER OF AUTHENTICITY

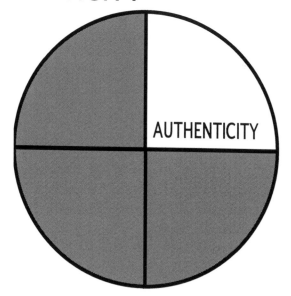

One of my first managers on Wall Street said to me, "I can teach you what you need to know about any product; however, I cannot teach you how to sell. You either can or you can't. The ability to sell is something that you are innately born with, and you either have it or you don't."

There are many people in the world that sit in this camp, and early on in my career, I believed that as well. As a sales professional, I never questioned whether I "had it" or not. I knew my outgoing personality, my persuasive skills and storytelling ability were all assets that enabled me to sell and sell well. My sales numbers and successful results confirmed that I "had it."

As I progressed and matured into roles where I was leading sales teams and leading a winning lineup, I looked for similar characteristics in other sales professionals that I had. I'd recruit and pursue people with similar characteristics to work on my sales teams. And during this run, I never actually felt I was teaching anyone who worked for me how to sell. I might educate them about a product or other industry related activities enabling them to be more prepared. But, I never concerned myself with training or coaching them how actually to sell, because I didn't believe it could be taught. At that time, I truly believed that.

I believed how to sell was unteachable until Sean Cosky was placed on my sales team. Sean Cosky was a member of a special analytical team on our trading floor which worked with very complex financial derivative solutions. Sean was a cross between an analytical Wall Street trader and a technical market analyst. He earned his undergraduate degree from MIT and returned to the MIT Sloan School of Management to earn his MBA.

The special analytical team was an entity unto its own. This group had been doing extensive work with many of our firm's clients and generated very significant revenue. However, over time, and due to many organizational shifts, this group was to be incorporated into my team. Initially, there was some tension for two primary reasons. First, because this group previously had autonomy and now it was being merged into a larger group. Second, the group it was being brought into was a "sales" group.

The special analytical team would never consider what they did was "sales." They'd often say to others at the firm that what they did was "so much more than sales." They were providing "strategic solutions" that changed the course of the work they were doing with their clients. The special team considered that the regular sales team wasn't doing anything nearly as meaningful as what the special analytical team was doing. The majority of these statements came from Sean Cosky. He viewed being labeled a "sales person" and part of a "sales team" as almost insulting, demeaning, beneath him, and soooo not how he'd describe himself. For my part, what I thought a sales person looked, smelled, and breathed like didn't fit Sean whatsoever. He was reserved, introverted, and kept to himself. Yet, Sean Cosky was brilliant and incredibly innovative.

At least on the surface, the incorporation of Sean's analytical team into my sales team appeared problematic. However, it initiated a change in my beliefs, altered how I view relationships, and helped me identify the true linchpin of one's connecting core.

Every so often, good sales managers will work with their teams to identify how they can expand sales production with a specific client. The manager will urge the team to go deeper, do more work, become more exclusive and uncover more opportunities. Referring back to our visuals, we're trying to bring our two worlds closer together. When the special analytical group merged with my team, I sat down with each sales person on the entire sales team to assess every client relationship we had. This included conversations with the clients in order to really understand the value each sales person brought to the client relationship.

After speaking with dozens of clients, researching for two months, and understanding our true relationships with each client, three things were clear. One, while many of the members of the original sales team had good solid relationships, they were just scratching the surface as to the potential they had with each client. Two, the members of the special analytical group, specifically Sean Cosky, had the deepest, most productive and profitable relationships with their clients. In addition, the client deemed their account coverage from this special analytical group as the key reason they did business with our firm. The clients could not imagine a world without working with them. And three, the top sales person on my newly combined team was a person who didn't self-identify as a sales person. I needed to better understand what Sean Cosky was doing.

After doing all the client analysis, I had my initial conversation with Sean; it was incredibly uncomfortable. It was uncomfortable not because he hated sales people, but my open and honest approach talking to him was not something he was used to hearing working on a Wall Street trading floor. I shared with him that I wanted to learn how he had developed such a strong relationship with his clients that they felt so connected to him.

Sean sensed my genuine interest and respect for him. He told me that his initial discomfort was because he believed that I was just an "unintelligent sales person who couldn't communicate on his level." Yes, those were his exact words—I wrote them down that day. He was beginning to see that I actually did have something between my ears, that I sincerely wanted to learn how I could improve personally and that I was being truly genuine and respected him immensely. As I recall, he didn't know quite how to react.

I shared with him some feedback from his clients. The comments, all positive, included such things as: "Sean's proposals not only worked, they changed the way we do business." "They were essential to our company." "Sean knows more about our company than we actually do." "We trust him implicitly and wouldn't imagine making a financial decision without him." After sharing these glowing comments, I asked Sean his secret to such great business relationships. Sheepishly, he said something to me I will never forget:

> "I don't know what I do or say to the client. I know I sometimes come off rude or insensitive, or geeky. I don't try to bullshit the client like some other guys in the sales group do. I've heard their style over the years on the trading floor and I can't do that. I only know what I research and study, and let my brain do the rest. I then speak with the client because I know I can help them. I don't know how to be anyone else, I'm just being me."

It was the most genuine thing I ever heard him say, and after he shared, Sean smiled as he saw my reaction. At this moment, Sean and I connected in a brutally honest way. It was powerful. My interest to learn was no different than the desire of Sean's clients to hear his ideas. Sean was being authentic Sean, and when he saw that I now recognized how valuable his unique style was and how much I respected him, Sean felt a connection to me.

Sean helped me see how powerful authenticity is. Reflecting on the adage, "You cannot teach someone how to sell. You either can or you can't," I recognized that may be true. One might not be able to teach selling. However, when it comes to connecting and establishing the meaningful relationship with clients that we strive to achieve, I beg to differ. The art of selling might not be taught; *the art of connecting CAN be coached.* If a strong, tight set of abs is the essence of a strong physical core, being authentic is the six pack of your connecting core.

HIGHLIGHTING THE POWER OF AUTHENTICITY IN A TOTALLY DIFFERENT WAY

So, while authenticity is a quality very important in sales and in the business world, the connecting core techniques which I coach can spread across many mediums. It relates to how one recruits and interviews for jobs, how one conducts family relationships, and even dating. Going on a date is in essence an attempt to make a connection.

When I first shared my story about Sean with a colleague, the two of us had a bit of a disagreement—about dating, of all things. Specifically, I believed that authenticity trumps all other factors when it comes to two individuals connecting. More specifically, I believed that if an individual is authentic, open, and sincere in a social or dating environment, others would find that person more attractive and would want to connect. My colleague did not agree with me.

Thus ensued one of the strangest social experiments in which I could ever participate. It started with a conversation over a beer at a bar in Austin, Texas and turned into one of the funniest weekends I've ever experienced. The question up for debate was, what would women find more attractive, a man's authenticity or inauthentic qualities, such as being more aggressive, being a little cheesy or more reserved. Let me clarify that by aggressive here, I don't mean physically aggressive, I mean extremely outgoing or forward or pursuing the initiative.

We had three good-looking, single men between the ages of 29 and 31 who were willing to participate in our experiment. We also took care to confirm the three didn't have significant others or girlfriends or any type of commitments. They agreed to go to bars, music venues, and other social places in Austin, Texas to meet different women. We set up the experiment so that the three of them would spend two nights playing three different roles. We planned for the test to occur during three separate sessions: (1) Thursday, at five o'clock, after the workday for most people; (2) Friday, at five o'clock, after the workweek for most people, and (3) later the same Friday night at ten o'clock. Each man agreed to play each role.

The first role was the aggressive type: extremely outgoing and very forward. An in-your-face type of individual who would have no problem going directly up to a stranger and asking them for information (like a phone number or email address), or asking if the person would like to have a dinner date at a future time.

The second role was the reserved type. This person would play a character that was very quiet and who didn't take any initiative to get the ball rolling. This role is opposite of outgoing or forward; the man would actually sit down and hope people would come to him. He would only speak if he was spoken to first.

The third role we defined as the "authentic archetype." We asked the individual to be the natural, authentic way that he was every day. In this role, our participants would open up and just relax. They'd be honest, sincere and the way they feel most comfortable. This might have included them being aggressive or reserved – we just wanted them to be themselves when in this archetype.

For the reader who is starting to wonder and get a bit curious about the purpose of this exercise, the goal was NOT to hook up with women. The purpose was to meet women and connect with them.

There wasn't a real clear-cut way to measure the success of this exercise. We decided if one of the targets, for lack of a better word, wanted to continue to follow up or stay connected with one of the gentlemen, that would be a successful connection. We defined follow up as an exchange of phone numbers, a business card, or emotively trying to speak to the gentleman again and continue the conversation.

My colleague and I decided we would be bystanders to witness as the three men went about role playing these three different archetypes during each session. In each hour-and-a-half session at the three locations, after the same number of minutes, each gentleman rotated roles, so each would have a chance to play the authentic, the aggressive, and the reserved archetype. After each session, we intervened to explain the experiment to the women. We then debriefed each woman separately, to learn their thoughts about their encounters with each man. The results, after a really fun and interesting Thursday and Friday night, proved one of the most unbelievable social experiences I've ever witnessed.

My colleague argued that the aggressive or forward male role would be most successful.

I believed that the authentic type would always prevail. At the conclusion of the experiment, the results supported my theory. The most successful individual was the man playing the authentic role, in every single instance. It was a nearly 100% success rate. When the participant played the authentic role, he connected, met, and had females interested to meet, if not that night, at another time.

Perhaps interestingly, the aggressive archetype placed second and, in our experiment, was fairly successful. Although, many of the women came back and said that they felt the "aggressive" was a little too forward. In last place, consistently across all three sessions, was the reserved archetype. Some women actually did try to talk with the reserved type, but our feedback session suggested that type made it difficult to feel a real connection with that individual.

In all three sessions, the authentic role player won hands down. Our favorite feedback from the debriefing sessions was, notably, that the women really were interested to learn what the men were like when they weren't playing the authentic role, so they could get to know them even better.

In the five o'clock session on Friday, one woman tried to meet the gentleman who played the authentic role. She had eavesdropped on his "authentic self" speaking with another woman and wanted to meet him. Unfortunately, the time expired and she never got the chance. At ten o'clock the venue changed as did his role. He switched from the authentic archetype to the role of being extremely forward. It turned out that this woman came to the third session's location, noticed he also was there, and sought him out. However, when she met him at this location she was very disappointed. In her feedback later that evening, she said, "This very authentic individual I thought was going to be interesting to me. Yet when I met him later that evening he was completely appalling and overly aggressive and turned me off immediately. I was truly disappointed as he wasn't who I thought he was based on my earlier encounter that night." When this woman learned about this social experiment, she shared with us how excited she was when he was being authentic and how disappointed she was to see him in the role of the aggressive archetype. I'm proud to say that three years after this exercise, that woman and the "authentic" bachelor she mentioned are married and living a very happy life somewhere in South Texas.

After the experiment with these three brave men proved my point that the power of authenticity trumps all when women are looking to meet men, my colleague continued to express his amazement at the results. While conversing with the three gentlemen who were the active participants in this experiment, one of them suggested, "You know, it would be really interesting to see [what would happen] if we flip the tables on this and you did the same experiment with three women."

After some detailed planning, recruiting and fine-tuning of the original exercise, we identified three women who agreed to participate in our experiment. The three women were equally attractive as the men and similar to them in age. Our three sessions were once again set on a Thursday and Friday night, at three locations where each woman would play all three archetypes, just as the men did. In this particular instance, the good fortune was that my colleague and I got permission from one of the locations to bartend so we could witness some of the conversations up close.

So, what do you think were the results of this experiment? To no surprise, at least to me, authenticity reigned supreme. Each of the women, when playing the authentic role, drew the men in. The surprise was the archetype that ranked second: the reserved archetype! The reason that it was surprising was not so much that the reserved was second, but that the woman playing the aggressive or forward role was last.

For some reason, we all had a preconceived "limiting belief" that an aggressive woman approaching a man with the intent of getting to know him would be more successful and that males would be more receptive to this approach. We were completely wrong. The results were staggering. The aggressive woman, while successful at times, frequently came across as being too pushy. Men had the same negative reaction to her not being authentic as the women in our experiment did to men. This may show that men might not be as shallow as we originally perceived them to be. When the men, unknowing parties to this experiment, participated in the debriefing session, they were completely stunned to learn the results uncovering their true personalities.

It is such an eye-opener to recognize the power of authenticity, to see how important it is for you to be YOU. So many questions arise as to why we sometimes feel the need to be someone we're not. Whether it's in a sales environment, where we might feel we need to be pushier or more aggressive, or some other situation, we must recognize if we utilize our power of authenticity, people will be comfortable recognizing us for who we are. It is the element of the connecting core that brings all of it together. Authenticity is our own strength of being that draws people to us. We might not always connect with people, but we can never know if we don't try. Without authenticity, all the other elements of your connecting core crumble. Authenticity is the linchpin to your connecting core and all your strengths.

BEING AUTHENTIC:

If a strong and tight set of abs is the essence of a strong physical core, being authentic is the six pack of your connecting core. One would think that there would be no work or effort required to be authentic. If you just are who you normally are, isn't that the most authentic version of yourself? Why would you need to do anything to be yourself?

In theory, this is true. However, I've seen numerous people attempting to be authentic who, due to the pressures of a situation, lean toward being something they are not. It could happen in a sales pitch or an internal meeting with company executives, or even a meeting with your boss to discuss a promotion or a raise. Sometimes, the preconceived visions of how we are supposed to be in these situations distract us from being who we ought to be ourselves.

BEING AUTHENTIC: BE OPEN

To be authentic, I remind myself of three things. Number one, "open." To share your true, authentic self, you need to be open. I'm not talking about pouring out your innermost secrets; I'm talking about sharing what's most important when you are connecting with someone. This starts by being physically open when you communicate. For example, in a face-to-face meeting, speaking while standing in an open stance is the first way to share your authenticity. Square your shoulders to the person or group you're addressing; have your arms at your side with your palms facing outward.

I actually begin most of my keynote speeches in this manner; it reminds me to open up to the audience. By doing this, you're truly opening up, and for a lack of better word, exposing yourself, which is kind of vulnerable. This is most effective if you're standing. If you're sitting in a chair, you can achieve the same effect. If a large table is between you and your target, try to move to a place that enables your open posture to connect. Minimize the distance between you and your target. If you can have a room with chairs and nothing in between, that would be ideal. However, since in most instances that's not the case, make sure to open up and face your chair directly to your audience.

This can feel quite vulnerable at first. You wouldn't believe how often I've seen people assume this open posture, and within seconds, cross their arms or turn to the side, thus losing that open position. It might seem silly or feel uncomfortable, but sharing your authenticity requires opening up. While you're connecting target might not first be as open as you, they will see and feel your willingness to be open, and if your message resonates with them, they will begin to open up as well. While this might sound hokey, being open enables your authentic message to flow freely, helping to draw you closer to your target's world.

BEING AUTHENTIC: BE HONEST

No matter how wide and open we stand, if we're to tap into being authentic, the message we deliver needs to be truthful and honest. If you're opening up your connecting core, reaching out to others, at the heart of it has to be truth and trust. Forthrightness and honesty are the building blocks to establishing a trusted relationship. The essence of being authentic when connecting with a new client, partner, or employer, all comes from who you truly are.

In instances when we're beginning to establish a relationship, especially in a sales situation, there are moments when we feel we might need to stretch the truth, exaggerate, or even lie to get in the door. While these tactics might lead to a sale or a promotion, or even a job, the odds are they're not going to get you to the true promised land of a *trusted connection*, and the power that comes along with that. When you open up, lead with the truth. Your targets will value and appreciate where you're coming from, and be more open to letting you into their world.

BEING AUTHENTIC: FROM THE HEART

If an open and honest approach is the volleyball equivalent of the "bump and set," when it comes to being authentic, then coming from the heart is the "spike" that forges the bond with your connecting target.

"From the heart" is an odd expression, similar to how "from the gut" or "deliver your essence" are terms that are difficult to capture. Other authors have addressed the value of coming from your "why," which I'll cover in the next chapter. We all inherently understand what this means, or what this refers to, whichever is correct.

As it relates to being authentic and strengthening your connecting core, it's the central message or point that comes from an open and honest place which will hit home with why your target should connect with your world. It will show your target how connecting with you will help your target benefit and grow.

In its simplest form, coming from the heart is the reason why you want to connect with your target, and how you can both benefit from the connection. To work on preparing and delivering this heartfelt message in an open and honest way, ask yourself WHY you want to connect with this person. The answer you come up with is the authentic "spike" you want to communicate to your target. Open, honest, and from the heart is how you'll be able to summon the spirit of authenticity to make that strong connection.

CHAPTER SIX

YOUR CONNECTING CORE: YOUR SUPER WHY

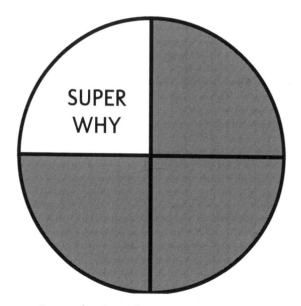

Growing up I was fascinated – or one could argue, obsessed – with Superman. Like many kids my age, I collected action figures and wore a blue-and-red-caped costume on Halloween, or any other opportunity I could find to wear it. I'd imagine having all the superhuman powers he possessed. Pretending to have super strength, freeze foes with ice-blowing breath, or staring intently at my younger sisters hoping lasers would shoot from my eyes. Any available bath towel was quickly wrapped around my neck to mimic his valiant red cape enabling me to take flight.

I even wrote a poem about Superman that was published in my elementary school periodical when I was in fourth grade. My parents were so very proud. I wasn't really a comic book fan so my initial exposure to the greatest super hero of all time began with the actual reruns of the famed 1950s television program, Adventures of Superman. To this day, I can recite the opening narration:

Faster than a speeding bullet, more powerful than a locomotive, able to leap tall buildings at single bound. Look up in the sky! It's a bird, it's a plane, it's Superman! Yes, it's Superman: strange visitor from another planet who came to Earth with powers and abilities far beyond those of mortal men. Superman who can change the course of mighty rivers, bend steel in his bare hands, and who, disguised as Clark Kent, mild-mannered reporter for a great Metropolitan newspaper, fights a never-ending battle for truth, justice, and the American way.

Aside from the fantastic nature of this mythical Kryptonian, I realized another major reason I celebrated him so much. While he was a fictional character, his persona embodied a true sense of purpose. He literally was put on this planet to use his superpowers to fight the never-ending battle for truth, justice, and the American way. This powerful credo resonates with so many of us because at his core we believed in what he stood for.

Author and innovative thinker Simon Sinek examines how inspiring leaders communicate, as he showed us in his first publication, *Start with Why*. He explains that starting from

Why establishes the core beliefs of your business. He believes that beginning your business communication here will enable you to inspire others. Many coaches, inspirational speakers, and sales and marketing experts have become devotees of the power of Why. Basically, Sinek developed the concept of the Golden Circle, which consists of three rings, from outer most to inner most. They are What, How, and Why.

Everybody knows what they do and some people might also know how they do it, but only a few people actually know why they do what they do. Relating this concept to sales, when talking about a particular product, we'd tell a target **what** the product is, **how** it is made and **why** the target should buy it.

Simon Sinek showed us that innovative and inspiring leaders actually communicate this in reverse order; they start from Why and work their way to the outside ring labeled What. Steve Jobs is the most commonly cited example of the power of starting from Why and its effect on how successful he and his company, Apple, became.

Jobs' vision, advertising campaigns, and entire company culture reflect his Why. Starting from Jobs' Why is how Apple actually sells. To quote their materials: "We think differently about everything we do and test the status quo with everything we make. How we do this is through an easy-to-use interface and beautiful design with every product we build." This is how Apple sells every single product that they make and it's their philosophy throughout their entire organization.

Does it work? At the time of this writing and for the six years previous, Apple is the largest tech company in the world. I'd say so.

The underlying principle of selling from your Why is something I have coached with many leaders and sales professionals. My concern is to transition these leaders from "what" selling – the what→how→why ordered format – and get them comfortable with "why" selling, formatted as why→how→what.

CONNECTING WITH YOUR SUPER WHY

Allow me to introduce you to Peter Michael, a longtime financial advisor to a major US wealth management firm. Peter used to introduce himself in the following manner, which I like to call "what" selling. Peter would begin, "I'm a financial advisor selling financial securities and planning services." Okay, Peter's method is pretty straightforward. Certainly, it's nothing earth shattering; in fact, one could argue it's boring.

Jema Valle, a former executive assistant, left her job to create a company called Date Night Planners, a business which plans all aspects of a date or special occasion. Initially, she described her business as "...a date night concierge service for very busy people." While this form of "what" selling described what her business does, when I first heard it, I thought she was possibly testing the limits of the law and that she was running an escort service.

I knew this wasn't the case, of course, yet the confusion was prevalent. To shift from "what" selling to "why" selling, we need to understand what is at the core of both Peter's and Jema's businesses. Only Peter and Jema know deep down why they do what they do. While others might have an inkling of understanding another's "why," the "why" must emanate from one's self. Each person needs to understand his or her own why.

Peter discovered his why in a situation that developed with one of his clients. He was the financial adviser to a 90-year-old woman, Dorothy Johnston. Dorothy was a widow, a mother of two, a grandmother of six, and a great-grandmother of four. When she sat down with Peter over lunch to discuss her financial situation, Peter became frustrated and very concerned for Dorothy. For more than a year, Peter had advised Dorothy that she needed to draft a will and testament and possibly create a trust to protect her family from a substantial inheritance tax burden upon her death.

Peter had addressed this matter for years with Dorothy and for years Dorothy ignored him. He explained multiple times how precarious her family's estate would be and what could happen to her children if she didn't properly address it.

Recognizing his methods were not working, Peter took a blunt tactic at that lunch. He said, "Dorothy, if you got hit by a bus after leaving this lunch and died, your family would lose a significant portion of your estate." Peter waited for a reaction and Dorothy responded, "Oh Peter, I'm not going to get hit by a bus any time soon."

Peter saw that even this harsh example wasn't penetrating and his frustration began to boil over. The truth was, he was still doing WHAT selling and wasn't coming from his WHY. While he always tried to maintain a professional demeanor with his clients, his true caring of her situation had hit a boiling point.

He leaned over, raised his voice, and exclaimed, "Dorothy, don't you understand? I care more about your money than you do!"

Peter described in detail how the headaches, stress, and financial worries of her descendants could be easily avoided simply by completing some paperwork. Contemplating this kept him awake nights. He truly worried about her situation; he knew how to fix it, but she wasn't enabling him to do so. Peter's true passion for his work and how he cared about the financial security of her family struck Dorothy at her core. By the end of that week, Dorothy had set up all the necessary financial papers to protect her family.

In addition, she held a family meeting to introduce all her descendants to Peter. If they weren't using his services at present, she wanted to make sure that they would in the future. Many of Dorothy's friends in her assisted living complex reached out to Peter shortly after that lunch.

One elderly woman called Peter and asked, "Is this the Peter that cares more about my money than I do?"

Peter had his WHY, and when you meet him today, he'll let you know it right away.

Jema Valle initially thought that she created her business, Date Night Planners, because she saw a need in the market. She saw that busy working men and women weren't spending enough time together and didn't have the time to plan a proper evening out with their significant others. Many of us know this to be true. Business can sometimes take over the life we want to live. Jema thought she created this service, Date Night Planners, because that's what the market needed. As it turned out, there's much more to it than that.

Jema Valle, if you saw her in person, is always smiling, always full of energy, and exudes confidence that's contagious. It's impossible not to have fun when you're around Jema. She's the life of the party, yet she wants everyone else to enjoy the moment as well. Most importantly, Jema is filled with a love which carries over to Date Night Planners. On the surface, DNP is a smart business that fills a need, but for Jema it taps into her WHY.

Jema believes in the power of love and the importance of spending time with the people you love. So while DNP takes care of all of the WHAT and the HOW of a date, at its core, Jema created DNP to address the WHY. Sure, DNP makes setting up a date, party, or special occasion easy, but at the center of Jema's WHY she's tapped into why you want to be with these special people in your life: because you love being with them. When it comes to strengthening your connecting core, and being a great connector, we not only need to sell from WHY, we need to own and embody our WHY with everything we do and every action we take.

So many generations appreciate and love Superman because we relate to his WHY. The Man of Steel's credo is a powerful and strong why: to fight the never-ending battle for truth, justice, and the American way. His character lives and breathes his beliefs in every episode, every comic strip, and every movie. As it turns out, Superman has yet another weapon is his arsenal, his "SUPER WHY." His spirit is goodness and fairness, something we all strive to believe in.

His SUPER WHY is his essence and is so strong we associate goodness with Superman. The "S" on his jersey embodies strength and confidence. His overall likeness we associate with hope. All of which makes the son of Jor-El and Lara one of our world's greatest connectors. Great connectors not only come from their SUPER WHY, they own it with every action. Your SUPER WHY should be the defining reason for your existence on this planet.

Steve Jobs lived his life by his SUPER WHY, thinking differently about everything and testing the status quo with his every creation. So much so, that his SUPER WHY has filtered down to anyone who has worked at Apple and anyone who feels special when they purchase an Apple product. Most of us do, admit it.

Peter and Jema are not only both incredible sales professionals as they lead with their WHY in the way they sell, they are amazing connectors because they embrace their SUPER WHY with everything they do.

Peter's actions, the way he connects with his clients, and how deeply cares about making sure they are financially safe and secure is his super power that draws people into his world. Jema's SUPER WHY, sharing the power of love and her passion for connecting us, is why people have embraced her business.

For the record, I don't plan any special occasions or events without using DNP because I believe in Jema's SUPER WHY.

Knowing your WHY is the first step towards strengthening your connecting core. If it doesn't come out initially or you have an idea but you're still crystallizing it, keep at it. Work with a coach if necessary to help identify your WHY. When you do, write it down in a book, a diary, or some special place that's easy to access.

To upgrade your WHY into your SUPER WHY, follow these steps:

Wake up each day and remind yourself of your SUPER WHY.

> Say it to yourself.
>
> Say it out loud.
>
> Own it.
>
> Live it.
>
> Breathe it every day.

Share your SUPER WHY with your colleagues, your loved ones, and even with your clients.

If your circle is uncertain about why you do what you do, make it part of your company's website, mantra, and marketing materials. Your SUPER WHY is your credo; it's your mantra that will draw powerful connections to you.

Just as Superman had the ability to change the course of our planet's direction, you and your SUPER WHY have the potential to do the same.

CHAPTER SEVEN

THE GOLD ZONE

You now understand how to strengthen your connecting core to draw in the worlds of your targets. You'll be able to establish strong, intertwined, and mutually beneficial relationships that can last for years, providing true growth and amazing potential. As the trust and deep understanding of one another grows, it leads to more business. Up to this point, I have focused on how you can connect to one specific target or company at a time. I've also simplified the playing field by zooming in on just you and your target. While this narrow focus is the best way to approach your target, it's certainly not the only way and not really what goes on every day. The images you've been seeing throughout this book illustrating your world and your target's world would certainly make things simple if there weren't many, many other worlds in your business universe. Your target's path would be unimpeded. There's an important world that we're already familiar with that comes into play and can help us with our connections. In fact, we're already connected to it.

The image above highlights a connected world that may have been a target world but became a **trusted connection** in our world. This new world, shown in our diagram, is a **connected contact**. A connected contact is an individual, group, or organization that knows, trusts, and intimately values your world. A connected contact is not only a relationship that is intertwined and connected to your world, but also has a very strong connecting core and draws worlds into its own world.

Over the course of our life and career, we've given this connected contact many names: family member; trusted friend; good client; reference; business associate; former employer; former co-worker; college friend, fraternity brother or sister; liaison; mentor; recruiter; coach; and there are other names you can add. Connected contacts can open doors to your world and expedite connections to your target. When the connected contacts have strong connecting cores and are master connectors just like you, the overlapping connections among the three worlds create a place that I like to call "The Gold Zone."

The **Gold Zone** is that overlapping area where your world, your target's world, and your connected contact's world merge. It's the focal point where the three parties understand one another. It's the place where previously established connections among each supersede formalities and provide a sense of calm and comfort. The Gold Zone is achieved when all three worlds realize the benefit of their connection. With this core connection, everything happens faster, flows more smoothly, works more easily, and even feels better. The combined power of these three worlds creates a vortex where there is clarity about what each world needs. These needs are understood and met.

It's difficult to demonstrate in two-dimensional images, but imagine that each world is represented by a differently colored ball of Play-Doh. If pressure is applied equally to them, they would form one ball with equal amounts of the three colors. This newly formed tri-colored ball represents The Gold Zone. The Gold Zone is a new level; it is not only the place you want to play, but where relationships develop faster between newly introduced parties and business deals are expedited. Less time is spent acquainting each other and more time is spent recognizing the power of the combined worlds. The Gold Zone embodies the ideal locale we strive to reach in the world.

The following three scenarios demonstrate The Gold Zone in action:

GOLD ZONE: *Tom, Julie, and Kim*

Dating can be very hard. There are so many individuals with so many interests in a very crowded playing field. It's hard enough to find the time to meet people, let alone meet the right people. It's the reason why online dating is a billion-dollar-a-year industry. Social situations, like dating, can highlight how effective and powerful The Gold Zone is. Take, for example, the story of Tom, Julie, and Kim. Tom and Julie grew up together, in the same town, attending the same elementary school, middle school, and high school. They had similar family friends. There was even a time when they tried dating one another, and while it didn't last, they remained very close friends. They went to different universities, but kept in contact. They'd see each other during vacations and breaks. After graduation, they relocated to cities on different coasts. While they weren't close geographically, they maintained a bond and tried to keep up their friendship.

Several years later, Tom relocated to the city where Julie resided. They met for drinks and dinner and caught up soon after his arrival into town. A few weeks later, Julie held a party and invited Tom. Since graduation, Julie had become very close friends with Kim, a co-worker. They eventually became roommates and for a time, were inseparable. Until Julie's party, Tom and Kim had only heard of each other. Julie often would comment how much Tom and Kim had in common with one another, and that they'd probably be friends if they ever met. When Tom arrived at Julie's party, he finally had the opportunity to meet Kim.

Julie was eager to introduce these two special connections in her life to one another. Julie had a gut feeling that they'd really get along well. When Julie introduced them, Kim commented, "Tom, I feel like I've known you for years." Tom replied, "I feel exactly the same way about you and I'm so glad that I finally get to meet the famous Kim I've heard so much about."

A few years later, Julie was maid of honor at Tom and Kim's wedding and toasted them, saying,

> "Kim told me that first night meeting Tom was the most comfortable conversation she'd ever had on a date and knew that everything would just flow and be easy from that point forward. They connected immediately and they just knew."

Stories like that of Julie, Tom, and Kim's happen so often that it's hard to dismiss them as pure chance. Bringing together your connected contacts yields amazing and powerful connections that elevate, expedite, and transform worlds. Here, Tom and Kim meet via one of their confidants. The Gold Zone is not an easy place to find. As in life, there are never any guarantees, yet there is such a higher hit rate within The Gold Zone than outside of it. All the traditional dating formalities weren't necessary when Tom and Kim first met. They already knew so many stories about one another from conversations through the years with Julie. The trusted relationship with the connected contact, Julie, fast tracked everything with Tom and Kim.

GOLD ZONE: *I worked with her back in the day*

Hiring good people is one of the most difficult challenges to building a great organization. Great leaders hire and keep great people and every organization forges their own culture with these great people.

I have been blessed to work at many different companies with incredible people. I've built an unbelievable network with many branches stretching across different industries, cities, cultures, communities, and areas of expertise. Like soldiers who go into battle with members of their company, the experience of going into the trenches of the workplace helps people form lifelong bonds.

At the turn of the 21st century during the dot com boom and subsequent burst, I worked with an extraordinary group of people at a digital agency called Organic. Although the company headquarters was in San Francisco, the team I worked with was in the New York office.

Organic New York grew at a pace that represented the mindboggling speed at which the early internet developed. At its peak, we spent more time saying "NO" to customers seeking our business than "YES" as we had to turn away opportunities.

Project managers juggled dozens of projects at the same time. Creative teams were pulling out all the stops and engineers and information architects were truly weaving the early internet sites of the World Wide Web.

The best way to describe the makeup of the New York Organic office was like making a very odd stew. Take some of the most talented creative artists and graphic designers, throw in some of the best computer programmers and information architects of the day, dash in some former advertising folks with a speckle of professional services and consulting leaders, almost all of them under the age of 30, and mix them together in one big bowl. Each day was amazing, intense, exhausting, exciting, drama-filled, fast-paced, completely nuts, and awesome all at the same time.

What came out of this Organic stew? I'm not talking about some of the most incredible branding work in internet design, nor am I referring to the intricate systems in worldwide implementations for some of the earliest e-marketers, and I'm not even addressing the millions of dollars of billable work that were generated from this very small office in Midtown New York City.

What resulted was a tight-knit group of people who trust, respect, admire and honor one another to this very day. The connections made at New York's Organic office were so well-established that after the internet burst and the company cut employees, the strong network remained. As these professionals took on new jobs and new careers and as other Organic folks looked for opportunities, The Gold Zone would come into play.

For instance, if a person was heading up an advertising firm's New York office and a resume from a former Organic employee arrived in the HR department, it was drawn into The Gold Zone. Organic team members were on board and hired as quickly as possible. Even years later, some Organic folks would reach out to me to inquire about places I've worked, and shortly after, conversations were taking place within The Gold Zone to see how these amazing folks could be on-boarded quickly. While due diligence, background checks, and job references are important factors to ascertain whether you're hiring the right person for your organization, when great connectors play within The Gold Zone, they will pair their connected contacts and speed up the entire hiring process. The results can be staggering.

GOLD ZONE: *LOCATION, LOCATION, LOCATION.*

Playing in The Gold Zone can speed up connections in your social life, your career, and employment. However, there is a no more tangible example of how The Gold Zone can impact your business and amplify results than in real estate.

The three important lessons in real estate still hold true. It's all about location, location, location. It's really all that matters. As it pertains to taking business to the next level, that location is The Gold Zone.

The venture capital community in Silicon Valley exemplifies this. Once an entrepreneur has proven he can create a success in a hot company, those who took the risk and came along for the initial ride will jump quickly at the next potential opportunity. They'll bring in other players to be involved. This is based on the level of trust and the proven track record.

There are countless stories of people who continue to invest in a player and then follow him throughout his career. One story in particular that highlights a truly successful place in The Gold Zone is where Marc Andreesen, co-founder of Netscape; Jim Clark, the Silicon Valley legend; and Jim Doerr, a partner in Kleiner Perkins Caufield & Byers, met.

In the early 1990s, Marc Andreesen met with Jim Clark, the founder of Silicon Graphics, who had recently exited the firm. Andreesen moved to California from the University of Illinois Urbana campus to work at Enterprise Integration Technologies. Clark believed the Mosaic browser had great commercial possibilities and suggested starting an internet software company. Soon, Mosaic Communications Corporation was in business in Mountain View, California with Andreesen as co-founder and Vice President of Technology. Mosaic soon became Netscape. Andreesen has often revealed how important establishing a connection with Jim Clark was, and how Clark's incredibly strong connection with John Doerr at Kleiner Perkins expedited everything.

The speed with which the initial money came in was amazing, as was the support of other partners and investors. The entire Silicon Valley community watched as Netscape launched at LIGHT speed. They raised more money, interest, and potential, which all stemmed from this very strong place within The Gold Zone, sparked by the trusted connections among Doerr, Clark, and Andreesen. The Gold Zone in action had these three strong, trusted connections all looking to mutually benefit from one another. The mutually beneficial value of this relationship is why they continued to collaborate on so many other ventures after Netscape.

Clark continues to profit greatly and to add to his legendary status in Silicon Valley. Doerr and his firm, Kleiner Perkins, made billions from their initial investment in Netscape and he continues to value Clark and Andreesen's views about other investments. Andreesen not only became a billionaire, but eventually launched Andreesen-Horowitz and has taken the playbook from Kleiner Perkins. His new firm has backed many entrepreneurs who move fast, think big, and are committed to building the next major franchise in technology. Andreesen is basically looking to find other places to make connections within The Gold Zone.

With trust, confidence, a deep understanding of your world, your target's world, and your connected contacts' worlds, the clear common goal is visible and shines through. The undiluted focus is on the only thing that matters: executing and getting results. If it's about raising money, launching a company, getting a job, or meeting a really amazing person, The Gold Zone is the place one aims for, strives for, and wants to be.

CHAPTER EIGHT

BELIEFS

Let's review; shall we? To become a Master Connector, we need to strengthen our connecting core. To do this, we need to:

1. Embrace the Power of Empathy, immerse ourselves into our target's world, and focus on understanding and addressing their needs.

2. Step through the fears that hold you back; cross into courage by spinning those fears on their heads, thereby attaining the Fearless Mindset.

3. Be Authentic by being open, honest, and coming from the heart with everything you do.

4. Unleash the power of your Super Why to draw targets and others to your world.

Through practice, repetition and routine, these exercises and actions will enable your world to attract targets and, in turn, strengthen and grow to achieve unbridled potential and capacity. Not only will you be positioned and viewed as a great sales person, leader, business driver, and networker, you will be seen as a force within your industry, community, and field.

While I've seen how a strong connecting core can launch individuals to new heights, can position companies toward uncharted territory, and can generate record-breaking results, a strong connecting core is NOT a guarantee that you will establish a connection.

A strong connecting core is not a foolproof way to bind tightly with other powerful targets. While a strong connecting core can bring worlds together, to really forge the bonds of these connections, one key component must be in place.

That key is like a gem buried deep within the center of your *safe*, within the core of your world. That gem is your belief system; your underlying, defining beliefs about how you see things, an underlying principle that has helped to mold and define who you are. Strong beliefs can lead to visions of how you view yesterday, today, and what tomorrow will be. Beliefs carry over into how we view family, business, politics, and religion.

When underlying beliefs differ, not only can it be difficult to connect with others, but in some instances, it can be a repelling force as well. For example, family strife due to opposing beliefs can create distance and separation. Disparate beliefs can lead business partners to part ways, corporations to split, business relationships to break apart and empires to crumble. Differing political beliefs can lead to arguments, fights, and even riots. Throughout human history, different religious beliefs have led to numerous wars and countless deaths. No matter how strong your connecting core is, if at the root of your world is a belief that your target doesn't believe in it, it's going to be very hard to forge a deep, lasting connection.

Take, for example, the Israelis and the Palestinians. They each have incredible Super Whys. They display their authenticity openly, honestly, and from their hearts. They are fearless in defense of their cause, and most of their leaders understand the plight of each other's situation. Yet, at their core, each side believes that the land beneath them belongs only to them, making it truly challenging to ever connect.

Dissimilar core beliefs can affect businesses as well. When core beliefs differ within a company it can inhibit a company's growth and development, potentially leading to its demise.

In the late 1980s I had the opportunity to work with a member of the executive management team at Eastman Kodak. In the early stages of digital photography and before the boom of the internet, social media, smartphones, and *selfies*, Eastman Kodak was the world's largest producer of photographic and motion picture film, a billion dollar company, a once proud member of the Dow Jones Industrial Average, and a brand synonymous with photography. The Kodak "K" could be recognized by almost half the world and in 1989 was one of Brand Magazine's top fifteen recognizable global brands.

At that time, I was working as a consultant, and my client, an executive member of the management team, was preparing to present the case to Kodak's board of directors for investing millions of dollars to develop their digital presence and to become an earlier adopter embracing digital photography. Many of the board members were unfamiliar with digital photography at that time. So much of Kodak's revenue and profits came from their strong hold on film. Aside from an upstart player in Tokyo, at the time named Fujifilm, Kodak was the significant brand across the globe.

In preparing this book, I dug up the actual presentation I helped put together for that client. On the surface and at that time, it seemed that digital photography was a perfect fit for Kodak since it gelled with the company's connecting core.

Although digital technology was in its infancy, it was the future. Kodak was the leader in capturing imagery; it's part of their Super Why. Our client saw this as the future and believed that was the direction Kodak should head in.

It was an authentic and open conversation that the company should focus efforts in this direction. It was fearless and aggressive. And I'd argue that the culture helped define the career of our client, who showed extreme courage to stand up to a ninety-year-old institution and present change.

Our client also had extreme empathy as the presentation showed that Kodak would sustain a financial hit initially taking on this endeavor; however, it would stay ahead of the curve and have a chance to maintain being a leader in photography. When my client made his presentation to the executive board regarding this opportunity, he observed his colleagues digest his idea and sensed the reaction was not necessarily positive.

After some internal discussion, the executive board told my client that Kodak had sustained decades of success in film and still believed that film was where their company should continue to focus. The board decided to not make digital photography the future focus of Kodak at that time.

Even though he believed that digital photography was where the company should be heading, and his idea seemed to match all the key components of a strong connecting core leading Kodak into the future, he couldn't connect with the rest of the board and the management team, because they had different beliefs.

They truly believed that film was, and would always be, the way people recorded their memories. They could not connect. He couldn't win them over because the underlying difference was in their beliefs.

Hindsight is 20/20, isn't it? We now live in a world where more photos are taken daily, without film, than were ever taken and developed on film in the history of Eastman Kodak. While the board of directors of Eastman Kodak in the late 1980s made a crucial error in judgment, connecting them to this concept was never going to happen. They just did not believe digital photography was where the company should focus its efforts. No one could connect to them until it was too late.

Some argue this was poor management and bad business. While this might have been the case, at that time, it was just against the beliefs of the leaders of the company. The connecting core, the S-A-F-E, can provide some form of compromise. However, a strong connection needs common beliefs to establish a long-lasting connection and to be able to merge the two worlds together, as one.

CHAPTER NINE

MAINTAINING A STRONG CONNECTING CORE

Having worked on a Wall Street trading floor for years, I recognized the holiday season 'twas the season for putting on a few pounds. Sure, everyone indulges a little more during the year-end session, yet, I'd argue that everything is amplified further on a Wall Street trading desk. Year-end breakfasts and lunches are ordered in, holiday candy baskets sent from clients and brokers are stacked on the desktops, and late-night drinking sessions take place each evening as the year draws to a close.

By the time New Year's Eve rolled around, I found my waistline to be a size or two larger. As the calendar turned over, resolutions were made to shed those extra pounds. To entice people to diet, bets were placed to achieve certain weight loss targets by the end of January. People would begin working out, dieting, and would eliminate carbs from their meals. They made sure they did whatever was necessary to win the weight loss pool and take home some extra money.

As impressive as it was to watch the dedication shown during January, the bad dietary habits were always back in full bloom by Valentine's Day. Maintaining healthier ways of eating always seemed to fall by the wayside. Maintaining your weight can be hard. So too can maintaining your strong connections.

With a strong connecting core, you can draw targets into your world, yet once you've established these strong relationships, how can you maintain connections? If strengthening your connecting core was burning off the fat and getting into shape, how can you keep the weight off?

One of the true strengths of a great connector is the ability to maintain these connections over time. Clients of mine who have learned about what it takes to strengthen your connecting core often ask me how I was able to maintain these relationships through the years. They wondered if there was a specific discipline that I used and could recommend to maintain core strength. I've always held that it takes hard work, focus, dedication, and stick-to-it-tiveness. However, there are three important steps that I was coached on from a very young age.

Like many boys and girls growing up in the New York City boroughs in the 1970s, basketball was a part of my formal education. Concrete school yards, metal backboards, and chain link nets were the fields of play, along with a leather ball. That's pretty much the only equipment that was ever needed. I was fortunate enough to have a basketball hoop set atop the detached garage in our driveway. Our house was on a corner, which made it a gathering spot for many after-school and weekend games. Year round, everyone who lived in the neighborhood would stop by and play. While I played often and learned from many of the older kids who played on the court in my neighborhood, I was fortunate to have my dad be my first coach.

My father truly loved the game. His passion for basketball, for the NBA, and especially for the New York Knicks, who were actually really good in the early 1970s, bordered on fanaticism.

His passion really came out when he would play with his friends or when shooting around with his young son. He was never overbearing and he wasn't one of those parents who domineered their kids like you might see some do today.

Looking back, I realize his coaching methods were very straightforward and simple. He really only provided three specific pieces of advice:

1. Keep your eye on the ball.
2. Follow through.
3. Stay between your man and the basket.

He reiterated these three points over and over so often to me, my friends, my sisters, or anyone who would listen, that they resonated and stuck. This advice carried over to any sport my father coached me in, whether the sport included using a basket or not. As clichéd as these coaching tips he offered were, when delivered with the passion and joy he felt for the game, they landed with impact. My father tried to incorporate his sports advice into daily life: Keep your eye on the ball, follow through, stay between the man and the basket. I recognized they actually do apply to so many other things. For me, personally, they related to my passion for connections, most specifically in how to maintain them.

KEEP YOUR EYE ON THE BALL

Let's simply substitute my father's word "ball" with the word "worlds." Keep your eye on YOUR WORLDS. As important as it is to make connections, it's probably even more important to track them. A master connector always asks him or herself what the status of a relationship is. They know the ones that are very, very tight. They do this by actually writing them down.

Great sales leaders utilize amazing software and applications for tracking pipelines. The same tools and upkeep are needed to maintain your strong connections. List your connections – all of them. Write them down and track the latest interactions with them. For the record, try not to do this in a spreadsheet. Get yourself a small notebook and write them in pen. Put them in a place where you can easily access them and update them accordingly. You should also track your connections' growth and progress. If it's a company, you should know their latest news and business developments; update them all and update them all the time. You need to keep track of your worlds like you're a satellite tracking activity and movement across the universe.

FOLLOW THROUGH

Dad was always referring to the motion of your arm when you shoot the ball or swing the bat or club. Follow through can be equated to FOLLOW UP.

The importance of staying in the loop with all of your connected worlds requires a proactive effort. The larger your network becomes, the greater the effort that is required to follow up. While doing mass communications is important, smaller scale communications such as newsworthy emails, holiday cards and wishes, or hosting large gatherings and parties to bring all your people together, the master connector follows through personally with those very important, valuable connections.

Individual attention shouldn't be given just for the sake of giving it. It needs to be an authentic and valuable conversation or meeting. Having a one-on-one conversation, ideally in person, with your connections several times a year is mandatory for maintaining strong connections. Try to connect once a quarter, if that's possible. Re-engage your power of empathy when you do have these connections. Make sure you focus on your connection. If your connection is also wise, they'll do the same and your session together will not only maintain your connection, it will strengthen it.

STAY BETWEEN YOUR MAN AND THE BASKET

My father always stressed the importance of good defense and the importance of being in the right place on the court. The basket always referred to the target. I don't think my father envisioned that his defensive mantra was going to be the linchpin to maintaining one's connections in the world and mastering the art of connecting. Yet, when you think about this basketball advice in terms of how you can maintain your position within The Gold Zone, you will see it's very relevant.

The Gold Zone not only requires three parties linking together on common ground and interests, where all parties benefit; it also requires each of these parties to maintain their connections with focus (*keep your eye on the ball*), and frequent follow up (*follow through*). Just as you need to stay connected to your targets, you need to stay in the space between your connected contacts and targets. Basically, you need to position yourself in The Gold Zone and work at valuing the connection you're helping to forge.

When you bring parties together in The Gold Zone, you can't just hand off the relationship. You need to stay involved. You need to make sure that all three parties are benefiting mutually. To maintain The Gold Zone, you need to have each party communicate proactively even through such things as dinners together, fun activities, coffee meet-ups, and drinks after work. The Gold Zone can only maintain its overlapping commonality if everyone knows their position within the zone and the importance of keeping these worlds together. My father would describe this as great team defense.

If you're fortunate enough to achieve a place in The Gold Zone, you must protect and defend it.

CHAPTER TEN

BRINGING IT ALL TOGETHER

All right, so let's review. In the beginning of this book, I shared with you that when I played connect the dots, the connected set seemed to have a greater sense of purpose.

Author Brené Brown defines connection as "the energy that exists between people when they feel seen, heard, and valued; when they can give or receive without judgment; when they derive sustenance and strength from the relationship." When worlds are brought together the give and take becomes mutually beneficial to both parties, enabling them to both grow and strengthen. Master connectors have the ability to draw these worlds together, and when they do, the power of the combined connection leads to amazing growth and results in personal, social, and business settings.

While some people appear to be born as natural connectors, all of us have the necessary internal components of a connecting core to become amazing connectors too. What I have tried to share with you within these pages are the exercises you can work on to improve your ability to connect with the targets you aim to reach by strengthening your connecting core.

You strengthen your connecting core by embracing your power of empathy. To connect with your targets, you need to stand in their shoes to understand their needs, worries, concerns and to get a perspective of what really matters to them. To unleash your power of empathy, you need both to ask and to listen. Ask the questions that solely focus on the needs of your target and listen, from Listening Levels 2 and 3, as a good coach would.

The next component of strengthening your connecting core comes from a fearless mindset. First, by understanding the fears that hold you back. You must listen for and recognize limiting beliefs. When you identify them, try to access what triggers them. Once you do, you can then move through fear into courage; spin the fear on its head and identify the gift in every fear. Use whatever triggers you need to adopt a fearless frame of mind with which others will seek to connect. If you have trouble doing this on your own, work with a coach to help direct you.

Be authentic. The connecting core's six pack is your power of authenticity. Being true to who you are is what makes your targets want to stick to your world. Flex your authenticity by being open and honest, and come from the heart when you communicate with your targets.

Seek to tap into your SUPER WHY. At the center of our connecting core is the reason why we exist on this planet. Our sense of purpose and unique abilities are our why. It's not always so easy to identify and it takes some digging. It might even take a coach to help draw it out of you. However, once you find what your Super Why is, recognize that it's your super power. It's the reason why other targets want to connect to your world. To unleash this power you need to wake up each day and remind yourself of your Super Why. Say it to yourself, say it out loud, own it, live it, breathe it every day.

Your Super Why is your credo and mantra and what will draw powerful connections to you.

Once you've worked on strengthening your connecting core, you'll connect with your intended targets and transform them into *connected contacts*. Those who have beliefs similar to yours will be drawn to you and you'll make valuable, life-long connections that will expedite growth and business partnerships.

Master connectors also have the ability to bring their strong connected contacts together in a place called The Gold Zone. This is an overlapping space where the combined power of your connections thrives and raises opportunity to a higher level. Once you've entered The Gold Zone and witnessed the power of strong connections and the upside of amplified results, you'll never want to leave.

To maintain your strong connections you'll need to work continually on the four core elements of your connecting core and remember to:

1. Keep your eye on the ball, maintaining and tracking your key connections. This will enable you to meet frequently with your top connections to stay on top of your connected world.

2. Follow through: Follow-up personally so you maintain your strong connections.

3. Stay between the man and the basket. To keep business within The Gold Zone, position yourself between your key connections and stay involved.

"We cannot live only for ourselves, a thousand fibers connect us with our fellow men; and among those fibers, as sympathetic threads, our actions run as causes and they come back to us as effects." (Herman Melville)

"Our ancient experience confirms at every point that everything is linked together. Everything is inseparable." (The Dalai Lama)

A client of mine once asked if there ever is a point where one's capacity to connect has hit its limit. Can a person be satisfied with the number of connections they have? To be honest, I don't know for certain. What I do know is that our only hindrance to connecting to everyone is our limited time on this planet and our limited accessibility to reach every individual on it.

I believe that our thirst to connect cannot be quenched. One who has mastered the art of connecting and sees the power that connections can bring will continue striving to make each of our worlds grow and develop. There will always be that urge to want to connect the dots and make lasting and powerful connections that can truly change our world.

Now you know how to do it.

ACKNOWLEGEMENTS

When I set forth to write *Master the Art of Connecting*, I had one major concern. It wasn't a concern about the content in the preceding chapters, rather it was the worry of making sure I appropriately acknowledged and thanked everyone in my *World*. I've lost more hours of sleep stressing about this section than one could imagine.

A disclaimer, however, at the outset-- there are many people to thank who will not be covered in this section. For those within my Connected World, you know that I'll make sure to thank you individually when we next meet. However, there are a few that must be recognized for how important they are to me.

To my family – my rock solid, trusted connections…

Mom and Dad, Bonnie and Elliot, the real "Dynamic Duo," thank you for everything. Most importantly, thank you for putting me on this planet and empowering me with a combination of your individual super powers—the ability to connect with and the desire to help others. It's a gift that I will continue to share with everyone I can.

Herb and Fanny, my father-in-law and mother-in-law, thank you for your unwavering support, for always being there, and for treating me like your own child.

My sisters, Melissa and Audrey, thank you for continuing our tradition from childhood of beginning our every conversation with a silly movie quote. Thank you for adding an awesome husband to your worlds; they have become the wonderful brothers I always wanted. And thank you for putting up with a wise guy, older brother like me for all these years.

To the team at BSP, you're all rock stars. Dealing with me can be challenging and you were all MORE than up to the challenge. Rob, John, Randy, Steve, Rebecca, Sydney and, of course, Burke, the "magic man," thanks for your patience and professionalism.

To Paul, thank you for helping me visualize and capture the unique way I see the World. You're a true friend and I'm forever in your debt.

To my "Connected Contacts," thank you for your endless inspiration and brutal honesty. I have always valued our friendship and only hope you have benefitted from me as much as I have from you. Every client I assist, business I help grow, and connection I make stronger, is a direct result of my connection with each of you. Your involvement in my life has helped me work with others to make them so much more amazing. In no particular order, thank you Isaac, Steve, Groo, Spiels, Baroo, Evco, Gargman, Carol, Zoom, Frischy, Sue, Liz, George, Ian, Laipps, Reis, LP, Duff, Joe, JB, Kristi, BNC, Cig, Kate, Hayley, Tami, Lou, Jamie, Jena, JP, Jen, Donna, Allen, Nisha, Fausty, Bison, SBE, Rob, Marc, Jon, Elaine, Billee, and Beth.

To Rocky, thanks for spending countless hours at my feet keeping me company as I wrote this book.

To my two amazing kids, Alec and Toby Kate, you are BOTH the inspiration of my life and every day you remind me that being a Dad is the best gig on earth.

And to my wife, Janet, I love you and thank you for always being there and believing in me.

ABOUT THE AUTHOR

When it comes to putting great people in touch with other great people, Lou Diamond is the master. He has over a quarter century of experience in sales, relationship management, business development and executive coaching. Lou's authenticity, energy and enthusiasm for what he does, along with his unwavering passion and desire for helping people overcome their fears and achieve their dreams, is unmatched.

If you're trying to find the right way to make the connections essential to building your team to achieve your business or personal goals, Lou Diamond is the man to help you make the connections to make it happen. Aside from selling everything under the sun for most of his adult life, Lou Diamond is an energetic, comical, inspirational, not-afraid-to-get-his hands dirty leader, business development strategist and performance coach.

Learn from Lou, who's been a top producer at every firm he's ever worked and has led sales teams to achieve record revenues year after year. He has consulted and mentored leading performers at hundreds of companies the world over.

He will send you on your way feeling as though you can conquer the world.... and make tons of great new connections doing it.

Made in the USA
Middletown, DE
31 October 2017